THE KITCHEN GARDENER

THE KITCHEN GARDENER

DAVID POPLE

WARD LOCK

First published in Great Britain in 1992
by Ward Lock Limited, Villiers House, 41/47 Strand,
London WC2N 5JE, England
A Cassell Imprint

Text filmset by Litho Link Ltd, Welshpool, Powys, Wales

Printed and bound by Dah Hua Printing Co. Ltd., Hong Kong

British Library Cataloguing in Publication Data
Pople, David
The kitchen gardener.
I. Title
635

ISBN 0 7063 6989 0

Frontispiece:
A formal arrangement of small beds edged with dwarf box are as effective for small vegetables as for the herbs shown here.

ACKNOWLEDGEMENTS

The publishers are grateful to the following for granting permission for reproduction of the following colour photographs: Harry Smith Horticultural Photographic Collection (pp. 8/9, 12, 24, 28/29, 36, 44, 48, 54/55, 58, 66, 71, 74, 78, 82, 93, 96, 101, 108, 112, 116 & 120/121); Photos Horticultural (pp. 18/19, 32, 62/63, 85, 88 & 104); and David Pople (pp. 40/41 & 116). The photograph on p. 2 was taken by Bob Challinor.

All the line drawings were drawn by Michael Shoebridge

Contents

Preface

It is the privilege of anyone with a garden to be able to grow their own food. None is fresher or more packed with vitamins, and since you decide how it is grown, none is cleaner. There need be no anxiety about spray residues, and if you want it to be truly 'organic', the method of production is in your own hands. What is more, you can choose to grow unusual kinds or varieties that are the best to eat, many of which you are unlikely to find in shops.

However, many would-be kitchen gardeners are put off by thinking that there may be a lack of space, that a vegetable plot must be an eyesore, or that it will involve a lot of labour and time. Yet one does not have to be completely self-sufficient for home vegetable growing to be worthwhile and even one large bed can be very productive.

As to appearance, throw away the old idea that vegetables are ugly and must be segregated. Where space is limited, integrate them as a part of the overall garden layout. By exercising ingenuity in design, arrangement of crops and keeping the area as tidy as one would a flower bed, such a plot can be ornamental as well as rewarding.

Some labour there is bound to be, but not an excessive amount if an intensive bed system is introduced to avoid treading on the soil. As for general care this often involves little, if any, extra work than would be expended on looking after the area if it were planted with something else.

In the following pages a fresh look is taken at vegetable growing in today's smaller gardens as well as larger areas. There are suggestions for ways in which vegetables can be woven into the garden scene, as well as different methods of culture from traditional to 'no-dig', and up-to-date advice on how to grow a very wide range of crops and suggested varieties. Also covered are the pitfalls and how to avoid them, and the use of non-chemical methods of controlling pests — information every kitchen gardener needs.

D.P.

SECTION I

Where gravel is used as a surfacing material adjacent paths need to have an edging to help keep the stones in place.

CHAPTER 1

Then and Now

At what stage the growing of vegetables became a distinct part of gardening is difficult to say. Certainly a wide range of crops was known and cultivated by the Ancient Greeks and Romans, and it was the Romans who are generally credited with the introduction of many of them to Britain. However, the production of vegetables in a kitchen garden as we understand it today would have come much later.

Early gardeners were chiefly, if not exclusively, concerned with growing herbs for medicinal and other uses. The few vegetables grown in villages were more likely to have been produced on a communal agricultural basis, and the common people probably relied mainly on plants that could be gathered. Land owners certainly developed gardens to supply vegetables and fruit for their estates and there are records of surplus produce being sold by their gardeners in London during the first half of the fourteenth century.

Enough evidence remains to suggest that quite a wide variety of crops was produced and enjoyed by the thirteenth and fourteenth centuries, but in the turmoil of the Dark Ages that followed, vegetable growing seems to have seriously declined. During this time, the monastic gardens were the main repositories of gardening expertise, and though their gardens were mainly given over to herbs, they did also grow some vegetables.

By the time of Henry VIII, vegetables were again popular, available in a much wider range, and by the end of the sixteenth century they were commonly grown by cottagers as well as in estate gardens.

As towns and cities developed, so did market gardens around them to supply the inhabitants with fresh produce. Away from such centres, anything of a quickly perishable nature had to be produced on the spot. There was no swift transport system to move such produce from one area to another.

Later, land enclosure meant the loss of open fields and, all too often, the loss of common rights that the country people depended on to produce their food. Finally in 1845 the General Enclosure Act laid down that villagers should be given quarter-acre field gardens to help alleviate poverty. Later still the Allotments Act placed an obligation on local authorities to provide plots on demand for town dwellers and others to rent for the production of food.

Through the ages the ability to grow food was an economic necessity for the common people and was frequently all that kept them from starving. A cottage garden, therefore, was more often a cabbage patch than the fanciful riot of flowers portrayed by Victorian artists. In rural areas this remained the case until comparatively recent years and there are still examples to be seen. There may have been herbs and a few favourite flowers, passed from one gardener to another as slips or plants, planted alongside the cottage or bordering a path, but the main area was devoted to vegetables together with a few soft fruit bushes and possibly one or two fruit trees.

The skill of raising vegetables rose to great heights in the Victorian era, when the widest possible variety was produced in walled estate gardens and techniques were adopted to raise fresh produce over the longest season. Land owners, together with their gardeners, would vie with each other in producing the earliest and best crops. Moreover, as the horse provided the main means of transport, manure was plentiful. Labour was also cheap and large amounts of both were expended to gain results that would be uneconomical today.

As the railways developed and offered a speedier transport for produce, market gardening expanded away from areas of population and their output was marketed in major centres. Later, road transport meant that it could be more widely distributed and fresh produce was offered in village shops also. The need for everyone to grow food in order to eat lessened, although some lower paid workers still found it an economic necessity.

Consequently home vegetable production again declined, though it was fostered at times by high prices and food shortages, and particularly by the 'Dig for Victory' campaign of the Second World War.

The rise in average spending power in the latter half of the present century, together with the increase in the value of building land resulting in new houses having smaller gardens, led to a further decline in kitchen gardening. Now, however, concern over chemical contamination by sprays and commercial growing methods, or just a desire to eat and enjoy the freshest vegetables and salads, has rekindled people's interest.

So today's kitchen gardener is more likely to be stimulated by the desire to produce healthy food than by any acute economic need, though he quickly discovers that home-grown produce can be far cheaper and fresher than anything sold in shops and markets. As well as drawing on the experience of generations of cottagers, he can also benefit from scientific research that has led to a better understanding of plants and their environment. This, used intelligently with improved plants, tools and aids, allows him to produce heavier crops with more certainty than was ever possible before.

Due to the generally smaller size of gardens today, the kitchen gardener often finds it necessary to explore more ornamental ways of growing vegetables and salads so that they contribute to the garden scene as well as produce a reward. He is, therefore, having to break new ground and adopt concepts largely unimagined by previous generations of garden owners.

CHAPTER 2

Good Looking by Design

Many would-be kitchen gardeners are put off taking the plunge and turning a part of their garden over to vegetables because they imagine they cannot devote enough space to the project, or that a kitchen garden would be unsightly. However, you don't have to produce all the vegetables and salads needed to become self-sufficient for it to be worthwhile. Indeed, very few people can afford either the space or time to do so, but it can be very rewarding to produce just a proportion of your needs, concentrating on those crops that give the best return, or are the most expensive to buy, even growing unusual vegetables that cannot normally be bought. A piece of ground no larger than 3.6 m (12 ft) by 2.7 m (9 ft), divided into two 1.2 m (4 ft) wide beds and run on intensive lines, can provide a surprising amount of produce during the course of a year if properly managed. There are also vegetables handsome enough to be grown among flowers elsewhere in the garden where they can help create what is commonly regarded as a cottage garden atmosphere.

As regards appearance, this is a matter of design and management. Although a kitchen garden area cannot compete with, for example, a bedding display for brilliancy, it is surprising just how much colour and interest can be introduced by the choice and arrangement of crops, to say nothing of herbs and fruits which can be woven into the scheme.

It has long been accepted practice to screen off kitchen gardens, largely because they have been designed and run on purely utilitarian lines. There is no doubt that an oblong plot with rows or blocks running north to south across it, is the most convenient arrangement for vegetable growing under traditional methods, though even this can be made more attractive by including a few 'useful' flowers and herbs. However, once you accept that it is to be made ornamental and included as a major element in the overall garden scheme, and that you are prepared to surrender to some extent ease of working and output for the sake of appearance, planning becomes much more flexible. Often the hardest part of creating an ornamental kitchen garden is in rejecting old preconceptions of what it should look like.

Although they are more trouble to lay, curved paths add an extra touch of class to the garden layout.

ORNAMENTAL OUTLINE

The first step is to create an ornamental outline that will set the scene throughout most of the year. This can be done by dividing the available area into symmetrically arranged beds by means of narrow paths. If the beds are no more than about 1.2 m (4 ft) wide, it is possible to reach the centre from either side without needing to tread on the soil. They can then be run on an intensive system that allows many vegetables to be grown close together to gain a greater output from a given area than is possible by traditional methods. Paths 30 cm (12 in) wide are adequate to provide access between the beds, but it is wise to use wider paths at intervals to make room for using a wheelbarrow.

Depending on the area available, the

basic outline can be anything from a circle divided into segments like a wagon wheel, to a square or oblong divided into small beds, perhaps including a central one, giving something of the effect of a knot-garden, parterre or a scaled-down version of the arrangement of beds in a traditional walled garden (Fig. 1).

This bold outline will have most impact from autumn to late spring, when the beds will be largely empty or contain small plants. In high summer they tend to be obscured and the plants will provide the major interest, though there is no reason why an attractive sundial, birdbath, lead cistern or even a seat or strategically placed tubs of summer flowers, should not be included in the design. Accent points of bright colour can be more effective than a large mass in attracting the eye away from duller areas, because of the contrast they make with their surroundings.

All paths should be surfaced to allow you to move dry-shod around the area at all times. Brick pavers and stone flags are serviceable, look attractive and are available in a range of colours. Gravel could also be used provided the beds are edged with wood or other material to stop the stones scattering on to the soil. On wide paths and broad areas, perhaps a site for a seat, it is worth mixing two paving materials to provide a contrast of texture and colour.

CHANGING LEVELS

A change of levels adds immediate impact to any garden layout and you can take advantage of this by raising some beds to a higher level. The very contrast of textures between walling material — be it brick, stone or wood — and any paving, can itself be attractive. The cost of supporting walls would add to the expense of the project, but can be worth the investment not only to add ornamentation, but for sound practical reasons.

Raising the soil level reduces much of the effort required, a point particularly appreciated by the elderly and anyone suffering

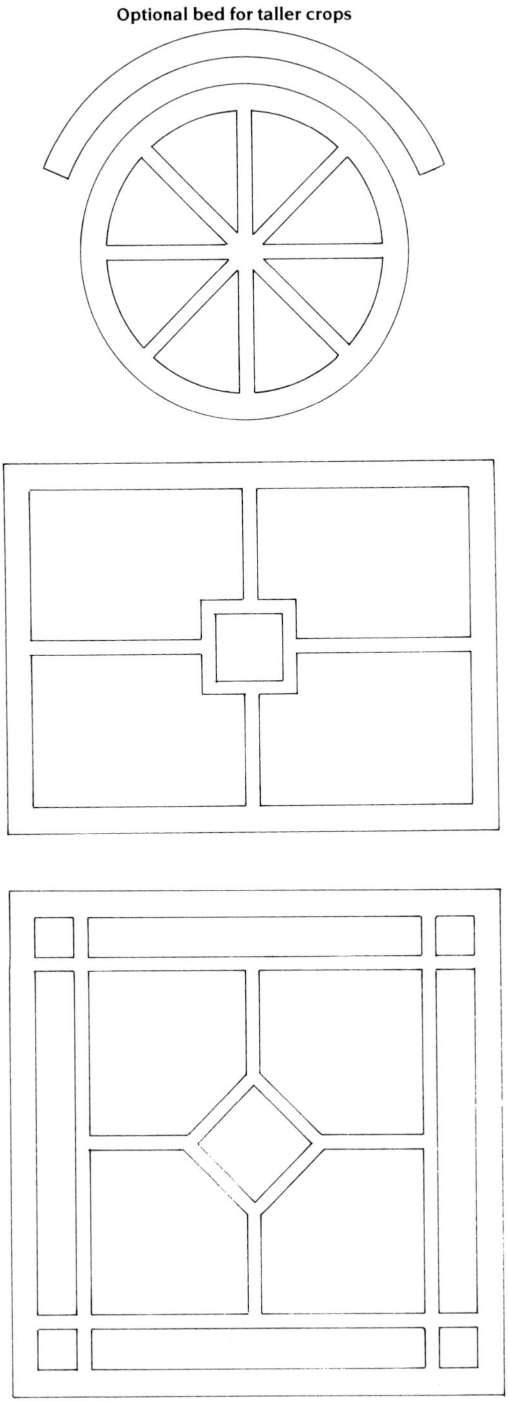

Fig. 1 *Dividing the area with permanent paths into manageable-sized beds imposes a strong decorative outline on the plot. Design is limited only by imagination, but should not be too intricate or access is difficult.*

from a back disorder. Where the soil tends to be clayey, as it is in so many gardens, surface drainage is also greatly improved. The extra soil required can be supplied partly, if not entirely, by removing the top soil from the path sites, and backfilling with rammed hard core. Such foundations can act as sumps to further improve the surface drainage of surrounding beds, which, having an extra depth of fertile top soil, have a greater potential for plant growth.

SURROUNDS

The surrounds of the kitchen garden must be taken into account in the planning stage. In a small plot, boundary fences or walls are likely to enclose it at least on two if not three sides. These can be clothed with climbing plants or wall shrubs, but a better idea is to adopt the practice of Victorian gardeners and use them for growing fruits, many of which are as attractive in blossom or fruit as ornamental plants. This will be more in keeping with the general food production theme. There are also climbing vegetables, such as trailing marrows and cucumbers that can be trained upwards in summer, which are attractive in flower and, in many instances, also when fruiting.

In larger gardens, flower borders can form the main surround, preferably separated from the kitchen garden by a wide sweep of grass or paving to prevent shade or root competition becoming a problem. However, if the colour contrast is too severe, such as could be created by a brilliant surround of

Fig. 2 *In this plan and perspective view, which could be part of a larger plot, the beds either side of the seat sheltered by a hedge can be filled with colourful herbs or flowers. Cordon and espalier fruit trees enclose three sides to form ornamental yet fruitful screens.*

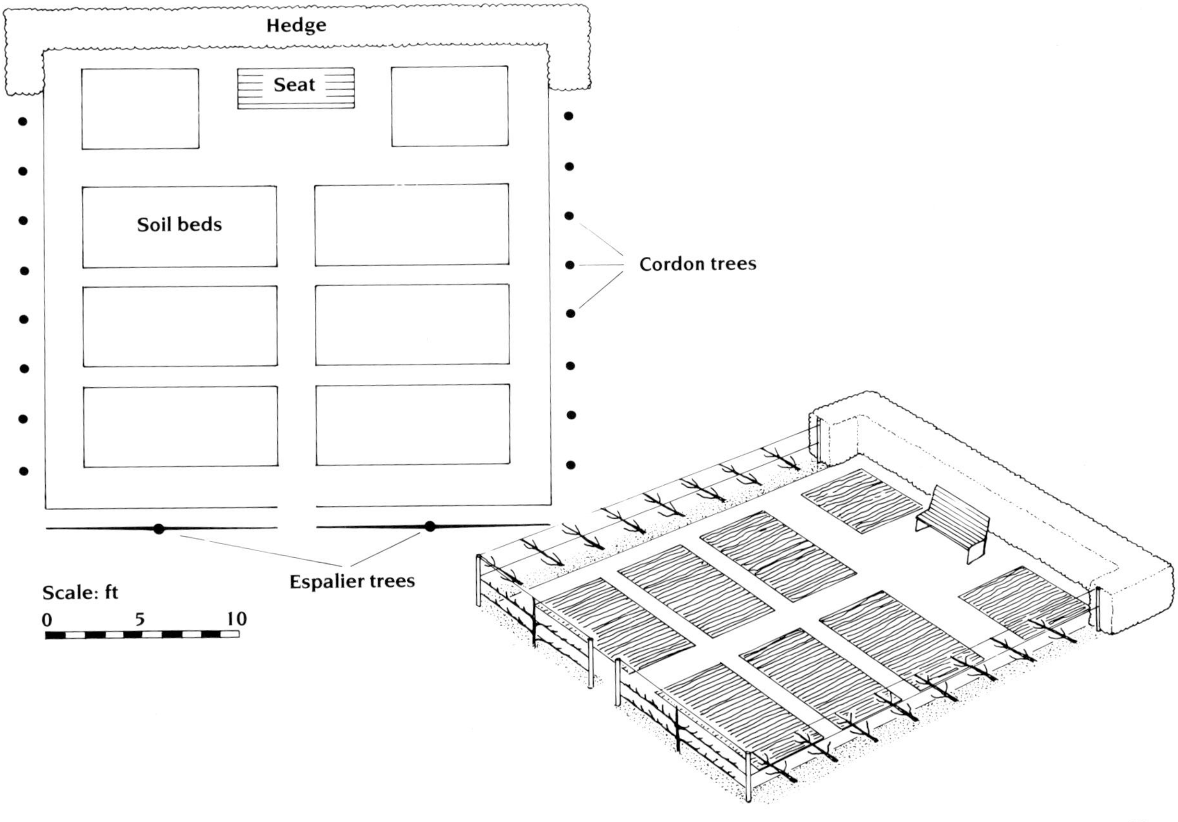

bedding plants, then the kitchen plot can look rather dowdy by comparison. Generally a mixture of shrubs and herbaceous plants is better as a surround in such a situation. Alternatively the vegetable area can be screened to create a garden within a garden, perhaps designed to give something of a formal courtyard feel (Figs 2 and 3), adding an element of surprise as it is entered.

Fig. 3 *Sheltered by a fence on the north side, here the area is divided into regular square beds, each accessible from a service path wide enough for a wheelbarrow, with narrower footpaths between. Note that space is available for a greenhouse and seat, and that ornamental paving would add interest to the scene.*

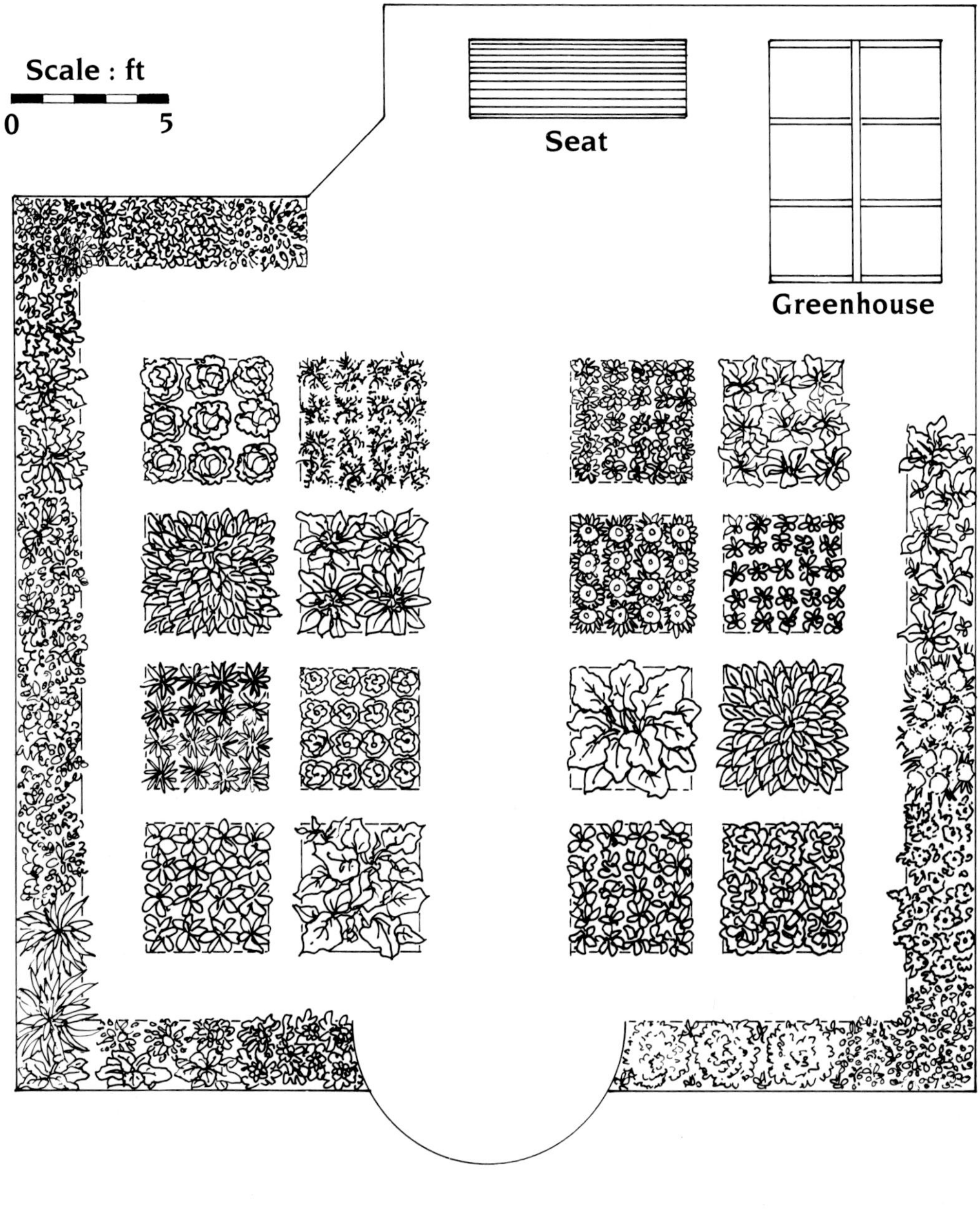

HANDSOME VEGETABLES

Few people stop to consider how handsome vegetables can be. Not many of them flower, but even quite common ones can make attractive foliage contrasts. The rich green, ferny foliage of carrots, maroon-stemmed beetroot leaves, brassicas with deep blue-green foliage and the pale yellow-green of many lettuce varieties, all add interest by way of foliage contrasts to the area. A number of the vegetables most suitable for small plots are positively ornamental.

Climbing beans, for example, make a striking show with scarlet, white or purplish flowers for many weeks when in full bloom. Particularly attractive are the red and white flowers of an old runner bean variety called 'Painted Lady', which has made something of a come-back in recent years.

Some varieties of dwarf beans are also very ornamental. The bush forms of scarlet runner beans, such as 'Pickwick', make a splendid show of red and, incidentally, seem to suffer less from the setting problems that sometimes afflict their climbing relations. Of the dwarf French types, the purple-podded varieties have attractive purplish foliage and flowers as well, while the golden pods of others, like 'Mont d'Or' and 'Wachs Goldperle', add a touch of sunny colour to the scene as well as being in the gourmet class for eating.

The huge yellow trumpet flowers of courgettes are attractive, as is the foliage of those varieties with silver-splashed leaves. There are varieties also with brilliant yellow fruits that add a bright splash of colour. Similarly many of the related marrows and squashes delight the eye first with their flowers, then with the colour of their maturing fruits ranging from cream to gold, particularly where trailing varieties are grown over a support or their fruits are raised above the foliage on blocks of wood or stone.

Seakale beet has very broad white leaf stalks that contrast well with the large dark, shiny leaves. The related rhubarb chard, with purple-tinted leaves and brilliant red stalks, is even more colourful, though has a tendency to run quickly to seed if sown too early in the year.

Lettuce includes a number of varieties that are colourful, some being red or tinged with red. Among the most ornamental is 'Salad Bowl', with pale green ruffled foliage, and its red-leaved counterpart. Instead of making heads these produce a thick ruff of leaves that can be picked as required. By alternating the colours in a row or bed it is possible to create an intriguing chequered effect.

Other vegetables that contribute particularly attractive foliage include the silvery globe artichoke, red cabbage, curly kales, purple kohl rabi, curled endive, blue-green leeks and red varieties of radicchio.

ATTRACTIVE HERBS

Not to be forgotten, either, are a number of herbs that are essential to any serious cookery and which could make a valuable contribution to the scene. Marjoram, thyme, sage, winter savory and rosemary all flower well, as will chives if allowed to do so. It is worth including easy-to-grow orange pot marigolds and red to yellow nasturtiums in groups or as edgings where their flowers will add a touch of bright colour for months. Blue-flowered borage also provides a long summer display.

Purple-leaved and variegated sages provide welcome foliage colour as does the feathery-leaved bronze fennel so easily raised from seed. Golden marjoram and golden balm both live up to their names with brightly coloured leaves and make a brilliant contrast against anything with purple tones, while the large-leaved lovage develops into a majestic plant with 90 cm (3 ft) flower stems resembling a king-sized cow parsley. Culinary parsley can be sown to produce an excellent edging to beds and borders, forming an attractive deep green ruff of curled foliage where it can easily be picked.

Although a kitchen gardener is primarily concerned with culinary herbs, there is no

An ornamental feature, such as this beehive, can provide an attractive focal point.

reason why some of the others should not be included for the sake of their looks or scent to make the plot more attractive. Obvious contenders for a place include lavender, bergamot, foxglove, opium poppy, honesty, catmint, monkshood and wallflower.

Such herbs and vegetables can be combined and positioned to make pleasing contrasts in a similar manner to a bedding scheme. It is all a matter of planning to get them in the right place. Such painstaking detail will add to the work in the first season or two, but where the area being dealt with is relatively small this is not excessive and the results can be both pleasing and eye-catching.

BORDER CROPS

Vegetables do not, of course, have to be grown in isolation. It is perfectly feasible to grow them among flowers in a bed or border; not, I hasten to add, quick-growing types like heading lettuce or radish, which would soon leave awkward gaps in the summer display following harvesting, but many of the cut-and-come-again vegetables that stand all summer, such as courgettes and seakale beet, as well as some of the purple and frilly-leaved kales, can be woven into the scheme to provide useful, if novel, foliage contrasts.

Alternating tripods of red- and white-flowered climbing beans could be used to give height to a border display. Although their flowering season lasts only about six weeks, there is the compensation of a delicious harvest to follow.

An obvious contender would also be the globe artichoke, with its ornamental foliage. This, in any case, is a herbaceous perennial that can be grown in the same spot for a number of years. So, too is edible rhubarb. Although the foliage of ordinary rhubarb grown for eating is not as striking as that of its ornamental cousins, a variety with well-coloured leaf stalks, like 'Cawood Delight' can make an attractive clump.

Apart from the loose-leaf lettuce varieties, like 'Salad Bowl', sown in late spring, few vegetables are suitable for use as edging plants. However, the perennial herbs, thyme, winter savory and chives, make neat border edgings and will flower in their season if allowed to do so. Spring-sown parsley will also make a neat edging, but should not be grown in the same place each year or it will become a martyr to soil troubles.

An exception can be made for borders normally viewed from end on. Here it is possible to grow any type of reasonably low-growing vegetable in 'bays' between taller flowering plants or shrubs (Fig. 4). From the viewing position, it is mainly the plants and shrubs that are visible and with care of choice and siting it should be possible to have a colourful display of flowers, yet still use up to half of the area for vegetable production.

A statue or elegant garden ornament sited at the far end would distract the eye from anything close to, and stepping stones can be used to allow easy access in broad areas to save treading on the soil.

FRUITFUL BOUNDARIES

Fruits can be worked into the scheme as well, not normally within the kitchen garden itself where they could cause shade problems and excessive competition for food and moisture, but trained over enclosing walls and fences. Alternatively they can be used to form internal fruiting screens or 'garden dividers'. Supports in this case could be decorative rustic structures, ornamental metal fencing or a simple support of posts and horizontal wires. By using only fruits that can be trained 'flat' against their supports they take up little lateral space and so cause no shade or access problems. Of course, if the kitchen garden is a large one, then fruits

Fig. 4 *This arrangement allows low-growing crops like lettuce, carrots, radish, endive and beetroot to be largely screened by low-growing bushy shrubs and herbs, such as* Lavendula spica *(lavender)*, Helichrysum angustifolium *(curry plant)*, Santolina chamaecyparissus *(cotton lavender)*, Euonymus fortunei *and* Berberis thunbergii *'Atropurpurea'*.

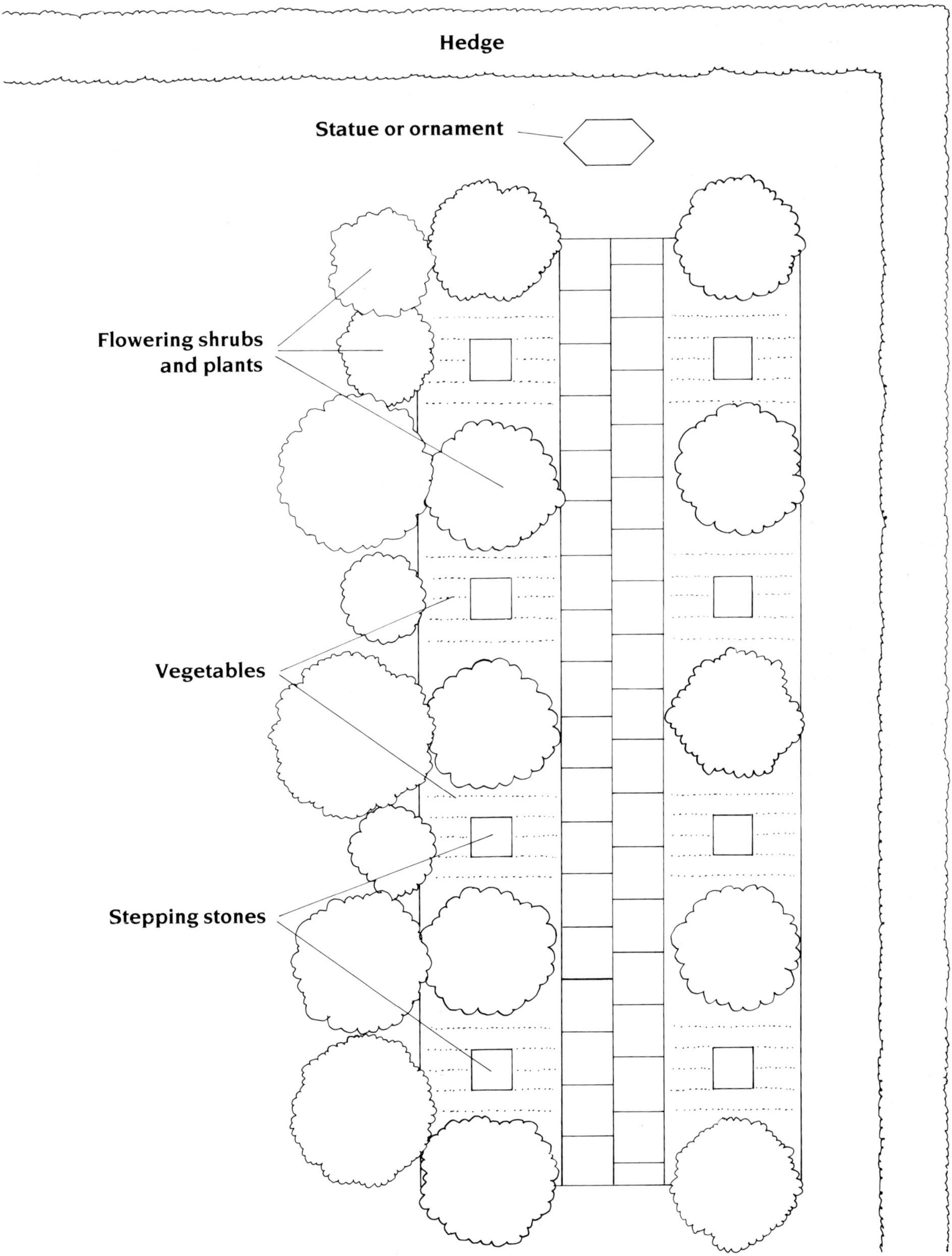
Hedge
Statue or ornament
Flowering shrubs and plants
Vegetables
Stepping stones

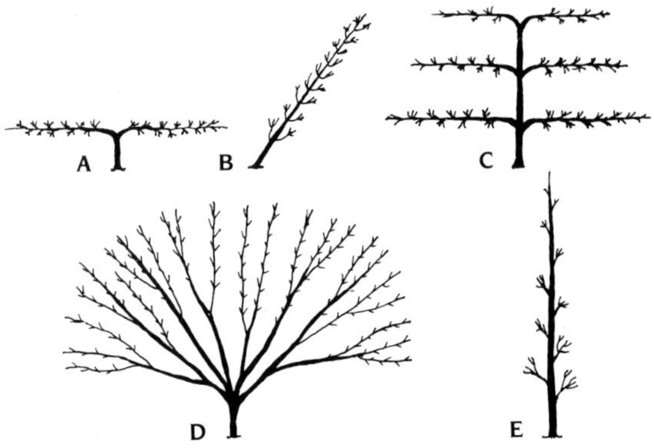

Fig. 5 *Trained fruit trees take up little lateral space, are decorative in outline and are particularly attractive when wreathed in blossom or carrying fruit. Forms commonly available are:* (A) *step-over;* (B) *single cordon;* (C) *espalier;* (D) *fan;* (E) *pillar.*

could also be trained on archways over major paths where they make highly decorative features.

Fruit trees are ornamental when in full bloom and their blossom is no more fleeting than that of their purely ornamental cousins. Many have a second, much longer, decorative period as the fruits strung along their branches colour and ripen in late summer and early autumn.

Apple and pear trees worked on dwarfing root stocks to control their size and vigour for smaller gardens, can be grown as single oblique cordons or espaliers (Fig. 5). Single cordon trees have but a single straight branch trained at an angle of about 45° and can be planted 75 cm (30 in) apart in a row. Espaliers have a number of pairs of opposite horizontal branches projecting from a central vertical trunk. Plums can also be trained as fans to increase the choice.

Apples are also available as 'step-over' trees, being trained with two opposite horizontal branches some 38 cm (15 in) above ground — virtually a single-tier espalier. Such trees can be planted to create a fruitful edging to the plot.

An unusual exception to the usual run of apple trees are the Ballerina and Minarette types, which are grown as upright cordons. These cast little shade and can be worked into the general design to form ornamental fruiting pillars.

The formal outline of all of these 'trained trees', as they are called, is decorative in itself from late summer, when they are pruned, through to late spring when their new shoots are again lengthening. They are particularly attractive when their branches are wreathed in spring blossom, while the summer pruning which they need to shorten the new shoots ensures that their fruits are well displayed and not hidden behind the foliage.

Among the soft fruits, those with long, lax canes like blackberries and loganberries are ideal and can be trained fan-wise or espalier-like along the series of horizontal training wires (Fig. 6). Since they have the same growth pattern as rambler roses they, too, can be trained as pillars by spiralling the stems of each plant around a stout upright pole. Set at intervals along either side of a path they could form an impressive, yet productive feature.

Red and white currants and gooseberries can be used also since, like fruit trees, they produce a permanent framework of branches that can be trained as fans or cordons — cordons in this case may have one to four upright branches. Gooseberries can also be

Fig. 6 *Blackberries, loganberries and other hybrids with similar long canes can be trained as fans* (A), *espaliers* (B), *or as pillars* (C) *where the canes are spiralled around a post.*

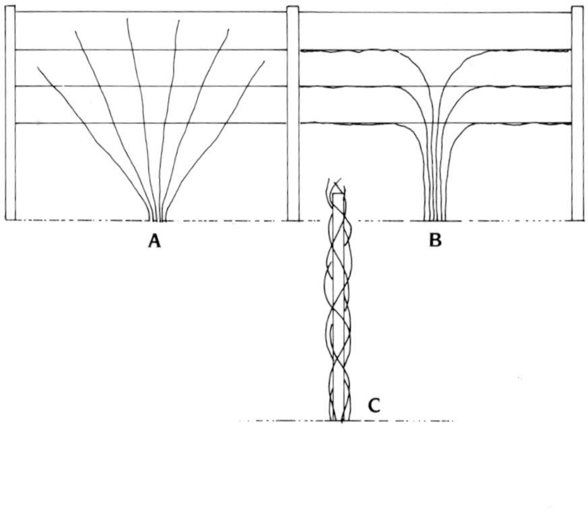

grown as standards, like miniature trees, with the branches radiating at the top of a short trunk. They could be set within the vegetable area to add novelty and interest.

Blackcurrants, which need to be grown as bushes and renewal pruned, and raspberries, that send out suckers in all directions, are better grown in an area to themselves, rather than try and combine them with vegetables. Strawberries can be fitted in with vegetables, but they occupy the same area for two or three years and are not a good choice where space is limited and the main aim is the maximum production of fresh vegetables and salads.

Although all these fruits can be trained flat, they do need considerable training space for development (Table I) and it is a mistake to cramp them. Lacking sufficient room they soon become a mass of uncontrollable growth and then give little or poor quality fruit.

Do remember to ensure that *all* fruit trees have suitable dwarfing root stocks. If not they will soon outgrow the site and become a perpetual nuisance.

GENERAL CARE

Where a kitchen garden is to be an ornamental as well as productive feature, it must be looked after in much the same way as any other decorative area, be it a rose bed or flower border, to keep it neat and tidy. You cannot afford to turn a blind eye on untidiness. Indeed a little extra effort is needed to keep the area spic and span.

Weeds must be suppressed, of course, but this can be of benefit to crops. Because the soil surface will be disturbed where crops are cleared and areas reused, which inevitably results in a fresh crop of weed seedlings developing, there will always be a need for regular hoeing. This should be followed by an occasional visit to remove any odd large weeds that are noticed, together with any yellowing plant leaves that could spoil the overall appearance.

It is unavoidable for some rows to become gappy where lettuce, cabbage and bunches of early carrots or beetroot are gathered as required, but this can be kept to a minimum by sowing often in short rows and clearing and refilling them as rapidly as possible. It is sensible, too, always to take a 'rubbish' bucket with you whenever harvesting. All roots, old leaves and other debris should be collected up and removed as the produce is gathered and the soil surface raked smooth before leaving.

Similarly, when main crops are completely cleared at the end of the season, remove every scrap of debris to a compost container and, if you are not ready to prepare the soil at once, rake the surface level.

Keeping the plot as tidy as possible really takes up very little extra time, but must be done if it is to look neat the year round.

One important point to remember is that vegetables — and most fruits too for that matter — need plenty of light if they are to crop well, so they must be given a reasonably sunny site. People who have failed in shady sites often ask what vegetables can be grown there. The only honest answer is none. If you do not have a suitable site it would be better to rent an allotment, or possibly obtain the use of part of a garden that is too large for the owner to manage, perhaps in exchange for any surplus produce.

CHAPTER 3

Forward Planning

The value of forward planning is under-rated by far too many kitchen gardeners. Yet it is essential if you are to make the most of effort and available space as well as arrange crops in the most decorative manner. It helps reduce periods of glut, when surplus produce has to be given away or wasted, and can improve output at times when vegetables tend to be in short supply and most valuable.

VEGETABLES

Personal Selection

First comes the selection of which crops to grow, and, unless you are blessed with unlimited space, this is inevitably followed by a process of slimming down the list to what can be fitted in.

The most economical crops are those which can be harvested repeatedly over a long period to give high output from the space occupied, together with any that are expensive to buy, and those which have a very short growing season, allowing the same area to be used twice, sometimes three times over, in a season.

Things to avoid where space is limited include such maincrops as potatoes, carrots, parsnips and onions, which occupy ground for a complete growing season and are freely available at a reasonable price. I'm not suggesting that you cannot grow better potatoes, carrots and onions than you can buy, but where space is at a premium, they are not as valuable as other crops. Asparagus is a similar case. You need to grow at least forty plants to get decent pickings, which takes quite a large area, but in this case it is occupied for upwards of fifteen years.

Among the best pick-and-come-again vegetables are runner beans, courgettes, seakale beet, perpetual spinach, calabrese, curly kale, and Brussels sprouts. Also snap peas which, because their pods are picked before the peas begin to form inside, continue to flower and crop over a much longer period than ordinary garden peas.

Quick-maturing crops include lettuce, radish, summer spinach, turnips and kohl rabi. Anything that can be sown in early spring and harvested by mid summer to allow the ground to be reused is worthy of consideration. Early potatoes, peas and broad beans, and carrots and beetroot gathered while young, come into this category. Worthy, too, are those crops that can be sown about mid summer to provide autumn and winter pickings, like winter radish, turnip and spinach, endive, chicory, Chinese cabbage, pak choi and many other Oriental vegetables.

Cropping Plan

The first step is to draw up a simple cropping plan – a scale outline of the plot on which the row positions and such details as plant numbers and sowing or planting dates can be pencilled in. This in turn should be divided into a number of sections of equal area according to the crop rotation that is to be used.

Organizing a crop rotation is a matter of grouping together similar crops, such as brassicas or root crops, and growing them

As well as being functional, the warm-coloured terracotta seakale and rhubarb pots add an ornamental touch throughout the year.

together. The groups are then moved, or rotated, to a fresh area of soil each season until finally they come back to the original site. Rotation of crops helps prevent the build-up of soil pests and diseases or other troubles particular to each group. It also allows the soil to be prepared to suit each particular group as well as make the most of the available supply of organic manure (Fig. 7). By the end of the rotation period the whole of the plot will have been manured and, if necessary, received its ration of lime to maintain soil fertility.

Group 1 Root crops	Group 2 Brassicas	Group 3 Other crops
Fertilizer only	Manure if available Fertilizer Lime If needed	Manure Fertilizer

Fig. 7. Three-year rotation. *By grouping suitable crops together and moving them each season they only occupy the same area one year in three. This helps prevent a build-up of soil pests and disease and allows the ground to be specially prepared to suit each group.*

The most commonly used vegetable rotation runs for three years, the three groups being:

1. Root crops — such as carrots, parsnips, salsify, scorzonera, Hamburg parsley and potatoes, but excluding turnips and radish.

2. Brassicas — all the leafy green members of the cabbage family, including savoys, cauliflowers, kales, Brussels sprouts and Chinese cabbage plus kohl rabi, turnips, swedes and radish.

3. All other crops — including peas, beans, celery, marrows, onions, shallots, spinach and tomatoes.

The area for root crops receives fertilizer only. They tend to 'fang' and produce a number of small roots instead of the required large single roots if grown on freshly manured land. That for Group 2 is manured if manure is available, fertilized and treated with lime if the soil is more than slightly acid. The ground allocated for Group 3 is manured as liberally as possible when it is dug and the food supply augmented with fertilizer.

In very small plots where brassicas make up a large number of the plants grown, then it may be impossible to create a sensible three-year rotation. In that case it is better to divide the crops into two groups: brassicas and other crops. Even a two-year rotation is better than none.

Where the aim is to grow most of the vegetables required by the household, potatoes could take up a lot of space and make a fourth group on their own so that a four-year rotation becomes practicable.

Although potatoes develop under ground they are not roots, but tubers. The crop will greatly benefit if the ground is manured. However, lime should never be applied where potatoes are to be grown. Not only do they prefer a more acid soil than most other crops, but lime encourages scab disease which disfigures their skins.

Having divided the cropping plan into sections to suit the crop rotation to be practised, the position of the rows can be pencilled in and the anticipated sowing or planting dates marked in the margin beside them. The plan now contains the basic information for all the major crops that are to be grown.

Catch and Intercropping

Two particularly useful techniques for increasing the output from a plot is the use of catch crops and intercropping. Catch crops are quick-growing vegetables grown and harvested from an area before it is needed for a major crop, or between the time a major crop is cleared and the end of the growing season. For example, winter leeks and most winter brassicas are raised in a seed bed and not planted out until mid summer. The area reserved for them would be wasted if left idle, but early spring-sown lettuce, spinach, beetroot, kohl rabi and dwarf peas can be grown and cleared before the land is required for planting the main crops.

Similarly, as broad beans and early potatoes are cleared, the ground can be reused immediately with sowings of lettuce, radish, winter turnips, winter spinach or a late sowing of dwarf peas for autumn use.

Intercropping is a little more tricky, but worth persevering with. It is a matter of growing a quick-growing crop between rows of a long-term one, where the quick crop can be harvested before the main one needs all the space or is likely to cast too much shade. Provided you know where the main crop is to go, it is possible to start off the quicker crop in advance to give it a better chance.

Lettuce and summer spinach are easily grown in what will be the spaces between rows of Brussels sprouts if they are sown early, or between widely spaced rows of peas or broad beans. They can also be grown along what will eventually be the path on either side of a runner-bean row. Dwarf French beans can be cropped either side of a celery trench on the soil that will eventually be used to earth up and blanch the celery. It is also possible to sow radish seeds very thinly along the same drills as slow-to-germinate parsnips and parsley. There the radishes not only mark the rows quickly, so allowing hoeing to be done early, but can be pulled and used before the other seedlings have done little more than appear.

Only the use of a detailed cropping plan, showing what is to go where, and when, will allow you to make the most of such opportunities.

The first cropping plan takes considerable time to draw up, but is something that can be done profitably on a few winter evenings. Thereafter it should only need minor adjustments each season to make improvements or to change the vegetables grown.

Apart from helping you to gain the greatest harvest from a kitchen garden, such a plan allows you to see what seeds you need to buy so they can be ordered in good time. You will also be able to assess the amount of fertilizer and lime required, so you need buy no more than necessary for each season.

It is always a good idea, too, to keep a rough diary in which to note down the crops and varieties that prove to be the most successful or enjoyable to eat, whether the amount grown was enough or too much, which combinations of plants look the most attractive and any other useful information. Such details can be invaluable when revising your cropping plan.

Ringing the Changes

Having decided on the particular crops you wish to grow, give special thought to choosing the actual varieties. Their worthiness in terms of cropping power and quality are important, of course, but so is their colour and appearance where the kitchen garden is to be ornamental as well.

The most suitable varieties are frequently not sold in packets by shops and garden centres, but have to be obtained direct by mail order from one or other of the major seed firms (Appendix 5). Most of these send illustrated catalogues, which are packed with useful information and make fascinating reading, free of charge on request.

When ordering seeds, do include one or two varieties that are new to you to try out. Some do better in certain soils and conditions than others. There are constantly new introductions, some of which are definite improvements on previous varieties and well worth experimenting with.

I am not suggesting you should switch immediately from a trusted variety, but merely grow a little of the new to see how it compares and assess whether a complete change would be worthwhile. If you always stick to the same varieties you will never see any improvement, yet some outstanding advances have been made over the years. Besides, trying something new does provide additional interest to the business of growing vegetables.

Trailing marrows and cordon trees trained over a metal arch with sunny rudbeckias along the base make a bright feature.

FRUIT

Selection

Although all the fruit trees, canes and bushes that are normally grown outdoors in a temperate climate are perfectly hardy, their blossom can be killed by spring frosts. When this happens they produce no fruit. They should not be planted in frost pockets or exposed positions where late frosts are common or cropping will be erratic. However, where the tree and soft fruits grown are trained flat they are easily protected.

Where the plants are trained against a wall or fence, a length of polythene, polypropylene fleece, hessian or other material can be attached above them during the danger period, rolled up during the day to allow pollinating insects to get to the flowers, and unrolled on clear nights when frost is expected or forecast. Trained against a post and wire support, the material needs to drape down on both sides, or can be pulled out a little from the base and pegged down at the base to form a tent, remembering to close the ends.

Apples excel in a cool, temperate climate, such as is enjoyed in Britain. Most pears do better in a rather warmer climate and will revel in the added warmth and protection provided by a sheltered south- to west-facing aspect. Plums flower earlier than either apples and pears and, consequently, are more at risk from spring frost, but otherwise should do well.

Most fruit trees need a mate — another variety that blossoms at the same season — with which it can cross pollinate. Even self-fertile varieties that can set some fruit with their own pollen, produce better crops when cross-pollinated. If you live in an area where there are plenty of fruit trees this is unlikely to be a problem. Elsewhere it is wise to plant at least two compatible varieties of any fruit tree and this should be borne in mind when deciding which to grow. All reputable suppliers will recommend suitable varieties to grow together.

All apples are compatible, but some varieties (the triploids) produce useless pollen. Where a triploid is chosen, therefore, at least two ordinary varieties should be grown as well so that they can cross pollinate each other as well as with the triploid.

Pears crop better for having a suitable pollination mate, but if you are restricted to a single tree, 'Conference' is capable of setting quite good crops unaided, though some of them may be banana-shaped if improperly pollinated.

There are a number of self-fertile plums that will crop when grown alone, but the best for a small garden is 'Victoria' (late summer), a good dual-purpose variety that can be eaten as dessert or used for cooking and bottling.

All soft fruits are self-fertile so you can pick and choose without having to worry about pollination problems.

Colourful Varieties

Since the garden is to be ornamental, as well as productive, apples are an ideal choice. Many of the varieties colour well before they are ripe and hang from the branches until picking time to make a mouth-watering show in shades of gold and red. Most plums also have very attractive colour ranging from golden to purple. Pear fruits, however, do not colour up until they are fully ripe, except for possibly some reddening on the sunny side, and because they need to be picked before they are ripe they do not contribute much colour to the garden scene.

Of the soft fruits, red currants are very effective, the clusters of jewel-like berries shining brightly for a time as they ripen. Gooseberries thinned out and left to swell as dessert fruit are attractive and usually coloured from yellow to deep red depending on variety. Even the heavy clusters of shiny, black, cultivated blackberries, crimson loganberries and other hybrids can make an effective display, not forgetting that they, together with all fruit trees, have also produced an attractive display earlier with their flowers.

Root Stocks

All garden fruit trees are made up of two parts — the root stock that controls vigour and size, and the variety that decides what the fruit will be like. When making a choice of fruit trees it is essential that they should have dwarfing root stocks. If not they will take much longer to begin bearing fruit, be difficult to control and probably soon outgrow their allotted space. The vigour and size of a tree depends on such things as the richness and type of soil, pruning treatment, natural vigour of the variety and average rainfall as well, of course, but is the type of root stock that has the most important influence in controlling eventual tree size.

Suitable dwarfing root stocks for apple trees are M9 for fertile soil and M26 where it is average to poor soil or rainfall is low. It is best to avoid very vigorous varieties such as 'Bramley's Seedling' which will make larger than average trees on any root stock. Since the trees are to be trained to a restricted shape, avoid any that tend to produce part or all of its fruit buds at the shoot tip. Best are those varieties that readily produce compact fruit spurs along the branches.

The most common root stock used for garden pear trees is 'Quince A'. Another, 'Quince C', is slightly more dwarfing but only suitable for richer soils and higher rainfall areas. It is also incompatible with some varieties.

The best root stocks for plums are 'St Julien A', which is moderately dwarfing and suitable for average ground and drier situations, or 'Pixy' which is more dwarfing but needs fertile soil.

CHAPTER 4

Basic Kit

Anyone starting to grow vegetables from scratch will need to invest in some gardening tools if they do not already possess any. The basic kit (Fig. 8) is a digging spade and fork, rake, Dutch hoe, draw hoe, garden line, plastic bucket, watering-can, garden trowel and possibly a dibber for planting. To these can be added measuring rods which can easily be made. Each of these has its own particular use:

Digging spade — essential for winter digging the soil and excavating trenches. I prefer the type without a tread at the top of the blade. It may be harder on shoes and boots, but is a lot easier to keep clean of adhering soil.

Digging fork — required for digging and breaking down clods, as well as such work as moving manure and lifting potatoes.

Rake — for levelling the soil and producing a surface tilth (a layer of fine crumbly soil) in which to sow seeds, also raking up debris. The type that has a head punched from a single sheet of metal is better than one with riveted teeth.

Dutch hoe — one of the most effective tools in the kitchen gardener's armoury for controlling weeds. It is used with a push/pull action so the blade skims just below the soil surface to cut the stems of seedling weeds.

The brilliant red stems of rhubarb chard make a bold splash of colour in among other vegetables and herbs.

Draw hoe — used with a chopping action to clear large weeds or earth up potatoes; also drawn through the soil to produce seed drills and furrows. The handiest design is what is known as 'swan-necked' where the blade is held away from the handle's end by a curved rod.

Garden line — used as guide when sowing or planting to keep the lines straight and in position. Two sticks and a length of string will do, but it is much more convenient to have a reel and spike.

Plastic bucket — for carrying fertilizer, water, small tools or collecting up weeds and debris.

Watering-can — for soaking seed drills before sowing, watering in seedlings as well as watering mature plants.

Garden trowel — for lifting and transplanting seedlings, sowing large seeds like broad beans individually, or loosening large weeds.

Dibber — essential for planting leeks and favoured by many for planting brassicas. A steel-tipped dibber is easier to use than a wooden one. Easier still is a foot dibber, easily made yourself by screwing a shelf bracket 15 cm (6 in) or so from the base of a broom handle. By treading on the bracket the tool is easily pressed into the soil. It can save a lot of blisters and bending if you have a lot of planting to do.

Measuring rods — two 2 m (6 ft) lengths of batten with imperial or metric marks. Ideal

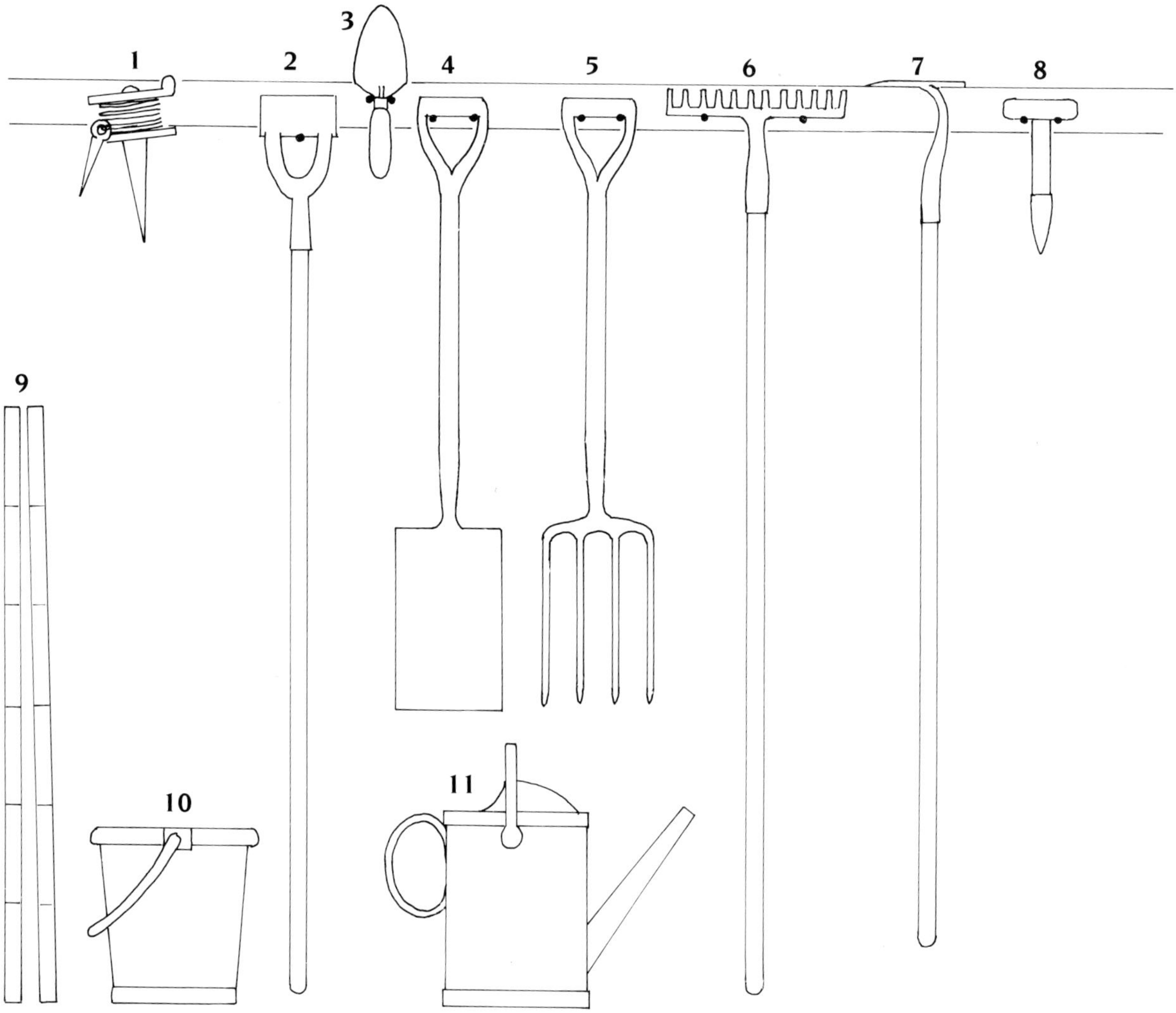

Fig. 8. Basic tool kit
1 *Garden line and reel*
2 *Dutch hoe*
3 *Trowel*
4 *Digging spade*
5 *Digging fork*
6 *Rake*
7 *Draw hoe*
8 *Dibber*
9 *Measuring rods*
10 *Plastic bucket*
11 *Watering can*

for measuring off correct positions of rows or plants within rows.

These are all that are really essential, but there are a few others that might be bought later if need or comfort make it worth while. My collection includes a weeding fork and a border fork, both of which can be handy at times when clearing ground, loosening a packed surface or lifting seedlings. I also have pair of onion hoes, small hand versions of a swan-necked draw hoe, and a manure fork which, with thinner, curved tines, is much more efficient than a digging fork for moving manure, garden compost or plant debris.

Tools are an investment, one that takes quite a lot of money, but as other tradesmen find, cheap tools are a false economy and it pays to buy the best you can afford.

STAINLESS STEEL

Most expensive of all are stainless-steel tools with plastic-sheathed shafts and handles. They can be a delight to handle and last for many years. Stainless-steel tools are not essential, however, though I would commend you to buy a forged stainless-steel trowel which really is worth the extra money for the wear and tear it saves on the hands. Stainless-steel tools also have a distinct advantage where the soil is clayey and tends to cling tenaciously to rough, and especially rusty, tools.

Well-made spades and other tools of ordinary steel are much cheaper, and, if looked after properly, will give good service. At the end of a spell of work, clean off all the soil from the blades and store the tools in a shed or garage where they can be hung up ready for the next time you want to use them. Do not leave them lying around in the garden, especially if they have wooden handles. It is also a good idea to wipe an oily rag over ordinary steel if the tools are unlikely to be used again for some time, to help prevent them going rusty.

Periodically sharpen spades and hoe blades with the aid of a file, and once a year rub linseed oil into wooden handles to extend their life. Such simple care takes very little time but will help to reduce work, make life easier, and save money.

CHAPTER 5

Ground Rules

Every kitchen gardener needs at least a basic understanding of what soil is and how to maintain or improve its structure and fertility. After all, soil that is conditioned to suit plants is the basis of gardening success and only flourishing crops will look handsome as well as be the most rewarding.

Ordinary soil is a mixture of mineral particles and organic matter containing moisture, air and a teeming mass of organisms, most of them microscopic. The soil can be good or bad from a gardening point of view, but the-less-than-suitable soils can be improved by careful management.

MINERAL FRACTION

The mineral particles — or mineral fraction of a soil — range down in size from stones and gravel through coarse sand, fine sand and silt to microscopic particles of clay. The quantities of the various sizes in the mixture gives the soil its basic texture, which controls the way in which it behaves. Thus a soil may be stony, gravelly, sandy or clayey.

Stony and gravelly soils are the worst for our purpose, tending to be hot and dry in summer and often having little natural fertility. Sandy soils are gritty to the touch, tend to be light, free-draining, warm up quickly in spring and are easy to cultivate, but dry out quickly in summer. Manure dug into them oxidizes rapidly and quickly disappears, which is why they are called 'hungry soils'.

Interesting variety is provided by silver-splashed courgette foliage, yellow green of the lettuce and deep green curly kale.

At the other extreme, clay soils are sticky when wet, heavy to work, slow both to drain and to warm up in spring. However, clay soils hold greater moisture reserves in summer and are potentially more fertile because of the minerals they contain and the fact that clay can also hold plant foods in the soil.

Most garden soils fall between these extremes, being a mixture of particle sizes, or what gardeners call 'loam'. Depending on the dominant type of particle, a loam may vary in texture from light and sandy to heavy and clayey. Best is a medium loam which contains sufficient particles of all sizes to offset each other's disadvantages.

ORGANIC MATTER

Under natural conditions organic matter is continually added to the soil in the form of leaves and other plant debris, dead insects, animal droppings and so forth. This is broken down by soil organisms, in the process of which plant foods are released and humus is produced. Humus is a dark colloidal material which is of immense importance. Its colour is what makes the fertile top soil darker than the subsoil below. Humus is not everlasting, however, and is itself eventually broken down.

Humus is important firstly because of its ability to improve the structure of a soil by encouraging mineral particles to group together into crumbs. These do not pack so closely together, so there are larger pore spaces between them. This improves both drainage and aeration. A good crumb structure is vitally important on clay soils, where the tiny plate-like particles tend to pack together, impeding drainage and aeration.

Humus is also valuable in that it can retain water, and any plant foods dissolved in it, to boost both the reserves of moisture and food for the benefit of plants. This is particularly valuable on the lighter soils that tend to dry out quickly.

Moisture is also held in the soil as a film around the mineral particles, the surplus draining down to the lower levels. When the particles are grouped together as crumbs, they are collectively able to hold more moisture than as individuals.

An important part of soil management, therefore, is the creation and maintenance of a good crumb structure. In gardening most of the plant products that would in nature enrich the soil are either removed in the form of vegetables and fruit, or cleared in the process of tidying up. The soil is also kept clear of weeds. Cultivations which improve aeration also speed up the rate at which organic matter is broken down. Consequently garden soil soon tends to lack the humus necessary for maintaining its structure and fertility and this must be made good either by digging in bulky organic manure or covering the surface with a layer of organic litter.

Stable and farmyard manure dug into the ground in autumn and winter have been the chief sources of humus for centuries. Nowadays proprietary precomposted manures, mushroom manure, hop manure and other products are available. Peat and bark can be forked in where the soil is seriously deficient in organic matter, to improve the moisture-holding capacity and structure but provide little, if any, plant food. Garden compost, made by rotting down soft organic debris in a heap or bin with the aid of an activator, can be as nutritious as manure when well made and is a valuable gardening by-product.

ACIDITY AND LIME

Depending on the minerals they contain, soils can vary from acid to alkaline and this can influence their fertility. Most crops grow best where the ground is slightly acid. It is sensible to test the soil of a kitchen garden before you start, and occasionally afterwards, to see that the acidity level is suitable and take steps to amend if it is not.

Testing can be done with the aid of a simple soil test kit or meter that can be bought in most garden shops and centres. Acidity and alkalinity is measured against what is called the pH scale, a logarithmic scale where the figure 7.0 represents neutral. Figures below this show increasing acidity, those rising higher increasing alkalinity. Most crops do best where the pH reading is around 6.5 to 6.8; potatoes at around pH 6.0. An exception are the organic, peaty Fenland soils where a level of pH 5.5 brings the best results.

Excessive acidity is easily corrected by dressing the soil with garden lime to sweeten it. Excessive alkalinity is not so easily counteracted, though dressings of powdered sulphur will help lower the pH for a time. Alkaline soils usually contain chalk, limestone or calcareous shell fragments and tend to revert to their natural pH level. Instructions with the kit or meter will indicate the amount of lime or sulphur to apply to bring the pH to the required level.

Lime contains calcium, which is a major plant food and this is being continually removed. The continual breakdown of organic matter gradually makes the soil more acid as well. So the pH status of any soil can gradually change.

The two usual forms of garden lime available are ground chalk and finely powdered hydrated lime. More ground chalk needs to be applied, but is longer lasting and best for light soils. On heavier soils hydrated lime is more effective. Both are best spread over the surface of dug soil in winter and left for winter rains to wash in.

Apart from its role in correcting acidity and providing plant food, lime is an important conditioner of clay soils. Like humus it causes the clay particles to group together to form crumbs and so improves the soil structure. A dressing of lime applied to a neglected acid clay can seem almost magical in the improvement it can bring to its workability.

Maintaining the correct pH status brings other advantages also. If the soil is too acid, the organisms responsible for breaking down organic matter can be seriously slowed down. Acidity also encourages club-root disease of brassicas, whilst an alkaline soil favours common scab disease of potatoes. Both extreme acidity and excessive alkalinity can cause essential plant foods to become insoluble and therefore unavailable to plants.

WEATHERING

We can thank the weather for acting as a third active soil conditioner, together with humus and lime, which is especially valuable on heavy soils. Where the soil is dug in autumn and left rough and exposed to the elements over winter it becomes much more friable. Continuous wetting and drying help shatter the clods, but it is frost which is the most welcome. The plate-like particles of clay tend to settle together and stick as tenaciously as sheets of wet glass, which are easily slid one from another, but very difficult to prize apart. When the moisture between the particles freezes and expands it forces them apart and upsets their alignment. They are then more responsive to the beneficial influence of humus and lime to form them into crumbs.

Fig. 9 *Where the area is too wide to reach from a path, standing on a board while working prevents over consolidation of the soil, especially where it tends to be clayey.*

The benefit of weathering is most appreciated in spring when raking to produce seedbeds, but it has an influence throughout the year. The improved structure is easily ruined, however, if the soil is tilled or trodden on while it is too wet. Always wait for the surface to dry sufficiently not to stick badly to boots or tools before trying to work the soil. In spring, work while standing on a path if at all possible, or invest in a scaffolding plank or two that can be used as a temporary path (Fig. 9). Apart from initial treading to settle the soil, such work as raking, hoeing and weeding is much easier throughout the season if you keep off the soil early on.

FERTILIZERS

Although plant foods are released by the breakdown of organic matter in the soil, most vegetables will produce better crops if this supply is augmented with a balanced fertilizer supplying more of the three major plant foods — nitrogren (N), phosphates (P) and potash (K). It can be an organic fertilizer, such as blood, fish and bone meal, or an inorganic fertilizer like Growmore. Occasionally it can be handy to use a 'straight' fertilizer, supplying just one of these major foods. Spring cabbages, for instance, will respond to a dressing of nitrogen in late winter or early spring to prod them into regrowth.

Fertilizers supply food in a very concentrated form and are sprinkled evenly over the soil, then raked or forked in. Care must be taken with their use, especially inorganic kinds, since an excess could upset plants, even kill them.

A base dressing of fertilizer is normally worked into the soil before sowing or planting. A secondary top dressing of fertilizer may be applied between rows of growing plants that need it, or they may be given secondary feeding by watering them with a liquid feed.

CULTIVATION METHODS

The traditional pattern of cultivation involves the digging of all vacant ground in autumn and winter to leave the soil open to weathering. In the process bulky organic manure can be added where required, annual weeds buried and perennial weeds rooted out, leaving a clear expanse of weed-free soil ready to prepare for sowing or planting in the spring.

As areas fall vacant in summer they are forked over, fertilized, and resown or replanted.

In old Victorian gardens it was usual to double dig the ground — forking up and working manure into the subsoil as well as turning over the top soil — every third year. This gave a greater root run for plants and increased the moisture and food reserves. There is no doubt that it had its advantages where there was no piped water for irrigation and is possibly still of advantage for a few selected crops, including runner beans, celery and perhaps cauliflowers. Whether the extra labour involved in double digging is warranted for ordinary home kitchen gardeners I doubt, and when the supply of manure is limited it is a mistake to waste it in the subsoil. I have not practised it for many years and still grow perfectly good crops. An exception has to be made, of course, where there is an underlying hard layer impeding drainage which needs to be broken up.

No-dig Cultivation

In recent years no-dig cultivation has gained in prominence. Under this system the soil is first double dug and heavily manured, then divided into 1.2 m (4 ft) wide beds separated by narrow paths. The crops can then be tended without standing on the bed.

The soil is not deeply disturbed again for years, if ever, but kept in condition by mulching with manure or garden compost which is mixed into the surface by worms or during the course of normal cultivations. The mulch is moved aside to expose the soil for sowing and planting.

Crops are grown in blocks rather than rows, the seed often being broadcast and raked in. The area devoted to paths is more than made up for by growing plants, such as carrots, beetroot and the smaller lettuce varieties, closer together in the beds which can give a much higher yield from a given area. The spaces between rows under traditional cultivation in many cases was merely to allow access for hoeing, weeding and harvesting.

A variation of this system is the deep-bed method where the top soil from the narrow paths between the beds is excavated and spread over the beds to increase the depth of fertile soil. This can improve the surface drainage of heavy soils dramatically. The sides of the beds can be permanently supported with boards or walls. The excavated paths can be filled with rubble and surfaced with narrow paving slabs or bricks. Alternatively the bed edges can be consolidated by treading when they will remain reasonably stable for a number of years. As they gradually erode, however, the edges eventually have to be rebuilt to regain the full bed width.

Such methods have proved to be very successful where the soil is not too heavy and the supply of organic manure and garden compost is adequate for mulching. Where the soil is very heavy, however, the supply of organic matter in the lower levels soon dwindles without fresh supplies being dug into the ground and root crops may suffer, though leafy crops such as spinach, lettuce and cabbages do well. Certainly the lack of soil consolidation by keeping off the growing areas is a great advantage.

It should always be remembered, however, that the more plants that are grown in a given area the greater the demand for food and moisture. It is essential to be able

Pages 40–41:
Summer flowers used as edgings and grouped within a vegetable garden make it much more colourful and attractive.

to water the beds thoroughly in hot dry summers, such as many areas of Britain experienced in 1989 and 1990.

Preparing for Fruit

Special care should be given to preparing any area for fruit trees and bushes, remembering that little can be done to improve the soil in depth once the plants are in position.

All the soft fruits recommended in the pages of this book, as well as fruit trees on dwarfing root stocks, appreciate a humus-rich soil that holds moisture during the summer, and one that is rather acid (pH 6.0 to 6.5). It should be well dug and manured before planting. Keep the manure below planting level. Fork peat or composted bark into the surface if the soil is sandy, clayey or lacks humus, together with a dressing of a balanced fertilizer just before planting.

CHAPTER 6

Good Timing

Timing is of the essence when growing crops to eat. Starting too early when the soil is unfit, or sowing too late in the season, can both result in failures when just the difference of a week or two can bring success. Where appearance is equally important we cannot afford to have gappy rows of seedlings or sickly looking plants. It is essential, therefore, for a kitchen gardener to work with nature when growing unprotected crops outdoors.

No opportunity should be wasted in starting off those earliest, most welcome, vegetables and salads. The controlling factors in early spring are the dryness and warmth of the soil. The soil must be dry enough to be raked to produce a fine surface tilth without ruining its structure. It is essential also for the soil temperature to be high enough for germination to be speedy and sure. If not, many seeds may rot and any seedlings that do appear will be sickly and fail to grow as well as those from sowings made a little later.

When a start can be made will depend on where you live, the type of soil, slope of ground and whether the site is exposed or protected. The milder the area, the earlier spring will come, but a start can be made on light soils before colder heavy ones in the same district. Similarly, a plot sloping at an angle to the sun will warm up before a flat one, as will a site protected from cold winds allow an earlier start than an exposed one.

The gay red-and-white flowered runner bean 'Painted Lady' shares a support with a cordon apple for a double harvest.

Evidence of weeds germinating is a sure sign that the soil is warm enough for sowing. Loosening the surface with a fork or tined cultivator to let in air helps it dry out and warm up.

Often there is only a spell of a few days early in the season when the soil is workable and every attempt should be taken to make use of it to sow such hardy crops as peas, broad beans, carrots, non-bolting beet, cabbage, lettuce and spinach, to have them ready for picking as early as possible. Miss such a golden opportunity and you could have to wait several weeks for another chance. There is always a risk of failure with such early sowings, but against the possible loss of a few pinches of seed is the extra value of produce harvested up to fourteen days earlier.

Sowings of parsnips, Brussels sprouts and other winter vegetables due to be sown in spring can wait until conditions are more stable.

Timing is again important when sowing the tender summer crops like sweet corn, dwarf French and runner beans. Seedlings of these can be killed by frost so you do not want them appearing until the chance of a late frost is over in your area. Sowings in late spring should be timed to allow for this. Again, if the weather is wet and cold at the normal sowing time it can pay dividends to delay for a time. Seedlings that get off to a racing start are stronger and can catch up with and often surpass those sown in unsuitable conditions.

The next important time comes at mid summer. The shortening days and reducing night temperatures after that period slow plant growth. To be certain of harvesting crops before the weather becomes too cold, final sowings of quick-maturing summer crops should be made then, together with those such as endive, heading chicory for autumn picking, and winter crops of turnips and radish.

EXTENDING THE SEASONS

In general the main growing season lasts six months from about mid spring to early autumn, but this can be extended by a month at either end by the use of cloches. These are low covers of clear plastic or glass used to cover rows or groups of plants to help trap natural heat to warm up the soil (Fig. 10). They should be put in place at least two weeks ahead of sowing time in winter to help warm and dry the soil ready for sowing. They can also be used to start the tender summer crops off earlier.

The gain in growth is due to the extra warmth, but because of shorter days and poorer light early and late in the season, plant development is not as quick as might be expected. Nevertheless, the use of cloches does result in consistently earlier and later cropping than would otherwise be the case. Spring sowing can be brought forward by a month; mid-summer sowings delayed for a couple of weeks or so until ground is falling vacant quickly as maincrops are cleared.

Fig. 10 *Plastic cloches, such as the County Cloche* (a) *or a flimsier but no less effective polythene tunnel cloche* (b), *extend the vegetable growing season.*

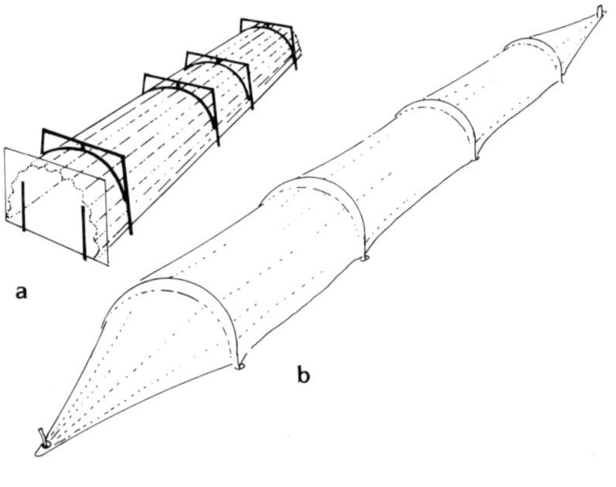

To gain the most from your investment, cloches should be used not for a single crop, but to start off several. Those used to cover first sowings should be moved in time to forward tender crops in late spring where they can be left in place as long as possible.

Move them again over late-sown summer crops in early autumn to keep them growing. Finally they can be used to protect winter vegetables, such as spinach and corn salad to keep their leaves clean, as well as spur growth in mild periods. Over-wintering plants and seedlings, including spring cabbages and early autumn-sown lettuce and spring onions, as well as late autumn-sown broad beans and peas that can suffer badly in severe weather, also benefit greatly from cloche protection.

GREENHOUSE AND FRAME

An unheated greenhouse or frame is also a great advantage to a kitchen gardener. There cabbage and lettuce can be sown in mid to late winter, grown on in individual pots and planted out at mid spring, preferably under cloches, to give hearty plants to cut before spring is over.

Other crops that can be forwarded in similar manner, or started off where the usual soil conditions make early outdoor sowings impractical, include peas, broad beans, cauliflowers and spinach. Such tender summer crops as marrows, sweet corn, dwarf French and runner beans can be sown under glass at mid spring and later planted out to gain the same advantage over outdoor sowings.

If the structure is heated, seed to produce extra large show onions and early leeks can be sown in winter, pricked out into individual containers and grown on before finally being planted outdoors. Additional warmth also makes it possible to raise tomato plants for outdoor culture.

FRUIT PICKING

It is essential to pick fruits at the correct time if you are to reap the full reward for your effort in growing them. In the case of soft fruits, it is a matter of waiting until they are fully soft and juicy. Do not be misled by the colour alone, which often develops before the fruits are fully ripe. This is especially true of some blackberries which, if picked when still firm but fully black, may be tasteless. The full flavour only develops with full ripening.

Similarly with plums. Wait until the fruits are soft, sweet and juicy before picking them for dessert. Those needed for culinary uses are usually gathered a shade under ripe.

Early apples can be picked and eaten straight from the tree. Later varieties should be left until they are ready to be picked then stored in a cool, not too dry place to ripen in their due season. The time to pick each variety is when the stalks of the fruits part readily from the spurs, when they are gently cupped in the palm then lifted and twisted slightly (Fig. 11). This will vary according to variety and generally the later the variety the later the picking season — as late as the end of autumn in some cases. Even then it needs several visits at intervals to each tree to gather all the fruits at the right stage.

Unlike apples, very few pear varieties will develop good fruit if allowed to ripen on the tree. These, too, should be gathered when their stalks part readily from the tree — this will mean several visits to get them all at the right stage. At this time most will be hard and green, even woody if they are late-keeping varieties.

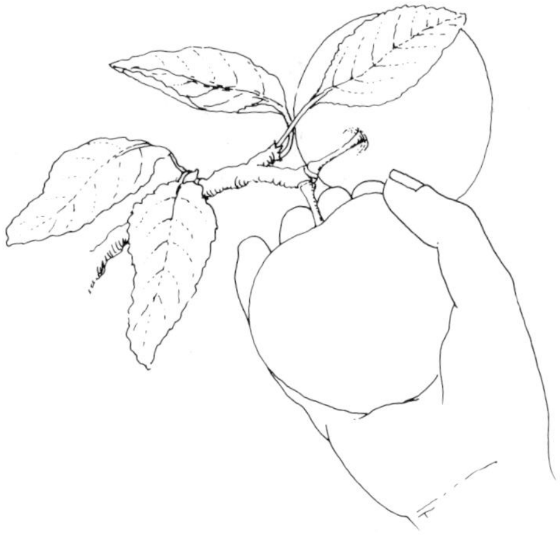

Fig. 11 *Apples are ready for picking when they part readily from the spurs if cupped in the palm, lifted up and gently twisted.*

The pears must then be stored in a cool, not over dry place until they begin to ripen, usually indicated by a softening at the stalk end and a slight change in the colour. They should then be brought into a warm place for a few days to finish ripening. The picking time is critical. If gathered too soon the fruits never develop a good flavour and often shrivel: harvested too late they tend to become mealy at the centre or gritty textured instead of being smooth and melting. One of the reasons why so few kitchen gardeners grow or enjoy many pears is the failure to appreciate this essential fact.

CHAPTER 7

Growing Concerns

There is nothing really difficult about growing one's own vegetables and fruit, but there are a few basic techniques that the kitchen gardener must learn if he or she is to be successful. Seed sowing, for instance, is basic to the vast majority of vegetable crops grown, yet it is an operation that seems to result in a surprising number of failures. Nothing will detract more from an ornamental kitchen garden than patchy rows or sickly looking plants.

In order to germinate, most vegetable seeds need warmth, moisture and a supply of oxygen. The seeds themselves contain enough concentrated food to see the seedlings through the initial germination period. Warmth, supplied by the sun, and oxygen are assured if the soil is friable and the seeds are near the surface. Moisture they absorb by contact with the soil.

A common cause of germination failure early in the year is too wet or too cold a soil. In summer, dryness is the usual problem, the soil either being too dry to stimulate germination or drying out during the critical germination period. Failure to create a good seed bed can exacerbate all of these.

PREPARING A SEED BED

The ideal seed bed is firm and moist below with a narrow surface layer of fine crumbly soil — the sowing tilth. To create the necessary firmness it is usually necessary to reconsolidate recently cultivated ground. Before you start, roughly level the surface and break up any large clods. If the surface was left reasonably even when digging, this should call for no more than a few strokes with a rake or tined cultivator. The soil is reconsolidated by shuffling up and down with feet close together to tread the whole area. Such treading also helps by crushing surface lumps.

Any base dressing of fertilizer can now be scattered evenly over the surface, followed by raking to create the surface tilth, at the same time combing out any stones or debris that could impede seedling emergence. I find raking one of the least enjoyable gardening jobs but it does not pay to skimp it. Aim to leave as level a surface as possible to lessen the chance of puddles forming.

Where the soil is heavy, and especially early in the season, a single treading is usually adequate. Further consolidation could ruin its structure and make raking impossible. It also pays when raking to work standing on a path or boards for the same reason. On light soils it is possible to tread and rake several times without harm, if this makes the creation of a tilth easier.

If experience shows that your garden soil tends to form a surface crust after rain, which can cut off the supply of oxygen as well as prevent seedlings from pushing through, rake in a 2.5 cm (1 in) layer of fine, moist peat into the surface when preparing a seed bed. This is also worth doing on heavy soils which tend to be tacky and difficult to rake.

Colourful chicories can add touches of red and purple to the autumn display in a kitchen garden.

SOWING TECHNIQUES

Small seeds, such as those of carrots, lettuce, brassicas and spinach, are usually sown thinly along shallow furrows made by pulling the corner of a draw hoe through the soil (Fig. 12a). A depth of about 1 cm (½ in) is ample for most of these. Use a taut line as a guide when drawing the drills, keeping the hoe blade against it and one foot on the line to stop it being pushed out of alignment where the row is a long one. Aim to make the drills of even depth or seedling emergence will be erratic.

Scatter the seeds thinly along the drill, water well and then draw the displaced soil back into place and tamp it down over the seeds along the row with the back of a rake (Fig. 12b and c). This is important since it presses the seeds into close contact with the soil to ensure good moisture absorption, and firms the soil so that it will not dry out quickly, as would happen if it were left loose.

By scattering thinly, I mean dropping the seeds about 1 cm (½ in) apart. This is ample for most crops since the seedlings will be thinned out to a greater distance apart and allows plenty for 'misses'. Spring onions are an exception which are worth sowing a little more thickly. If the seeds are very expensive, or you want to make them go as far as possible, they can be sown in small groups where each mature plant will grow, but normally it is hardly worth the fiddle. Most packets of seeds contain ample seeds for one season's sowings.

An alternative method for closing a drill is to shuffle along it with feet splayed. The loosened soil is then funnelled back into place by your boots, while your heels will compress it again. However, the raking method is far better on heavy soils which can easily be over consolidated.

Fig. 12 *Three steps to successful germination of small seeds are to open a shallow drill with the corner of a draw hoe (a), flood it with water (b). If the soil seems rather dry, then tamp down the loose soil over the seeds (c) after refilling the drill.*

Moisture is one of the major keys to good germination. Should the soil seem rather dry, always flood the open drills with water and allow it to drain in immediately before sowing. Simply walk beside the drill directing water into it from the spout of a can (Fig. 12c). This will ensure swift and even germination along the rows in dry weather and save the need for further watering before the seedlings appear, except possibly for parsley which is very slow to germinate.

LARGE SEEDS

Large seeds, such as those of peas, beans and marrows, can easily be handled and sown individually. No seeds will give 100% germination, so they can either be sown in twos or threes where a plant is required and the surplus removed after germination, or a few spares can be sown between the rows for transplanting later to fill any gaps.

The traditional method of sowing peas is to make a wide flat-bottomed drill with the aid of a spade or draw hoe and space out the seeds about 5 cm (2 in) apart in three rows over the base. However, I find it far more convenient to make two parallel drills, 2.5 cm (1 in) deep and 15 cm (6 in) apart, and drop the seeds in about 5 cm (2 in) apart along them. Not only is it quicker and less laborious, but a hoe can be run between the rows when the seedlings first appear to control weeds and the crop is just as heavy.

Beans and sweet corn, which are quite widely spaced, are easily sown individually using a trowel to make the holes. If you find it difficult to judge the depth, either use a graduated trowel, such as is sold for planting bulbs, or simply stick a piece of self-adhesive tape the required height up the blade.

Seeds of marrows, squashes and other related vegetables are also easily sown individually. These seeds are flat, however, and it is a good idea to set them on edge so they are less likely to rot if the weather turns wet soon after sowing.

THINNING CROPS

Once seedlings are about 2.5 cm (1 in) high it is time for the first thinning out for those that need it — a simple matter of working along the rows and hoeing up or pulling out the surplus plants. It also makes weed control easier by allowing you to hoe between the plants as well as between the rows. Delaying thinning beyond this point not only wastes valuable food and moisture, but the seedlings begin to crowd each other and become drawn.

I prefer to thin in two stages early in the season, first to half the distance required then later, when the plants begin to jostle one another, to the final spacing (Fig. 13). At this stage the surplus plants of some vegetables, including lettuce and spinach, can go to the kitchen rather than the compost heap. Such thinnings can form the first, welcome pickings of the new season's crops.

In gardens where slugs tend to be a nuisance and take a heavy toll of seedlings, an extra thinning at first to 5 cm (2 in) apart can pay dividends. It prevents overcrowding for a while but allows for additional seedling losses to slugs without seriously reducing the crop. Such thinning is also an advantage with early sown lettuce where a proportion of the plants is to be transplanted, which cannot be done until the seedlings are a

Fig. 13 *By first thinning crops like lettuce and spinach to half the final distance, at the second thinning the removed plants are large enough to eat.*

little larger. It is then possible to dig them up keeping plenty of soil about their roots so they hardly notice the move.

Although many would consider it a council of perfection, I find it also pays to thin out brassica seedlings raised in a seed bed for transplanting to about 5 cm (2 in) apart as soon as the seedlings appear. This really does result in much sturdier young plants since they do not compete one with another for space and light. They too can be moved with a good block of soil around their roots.

Thinning is best done when the soil is moist, so if the weather is dry, water the rows the day before. At each stage of thinning also take the opportunity to pull out any weeds growing around the plants.

FEEDING

All plants take up a variety of foods from the soil. A little is derived from minerals, much more from organic matter as it decomposes. Generally, however, plants can make use of more food than is available naturally and cropping is improved where these natural sources are augmented with a general, balanced fertilizer which provides more of the big three elements — nitrogen, phosphorus or phosphates and potassium or potash.

Each of these has an important role to play. Nitrogen is the growth element and is specially important for leaf and stem growth. It is also needed by the soil organisms responsible for the breakdown of organic matter and, being soluble, is the element most readily leached from the soil. Phosphates encourage root development, are associated with the movement of food throughout a plant and are important in seed development. Little of this element is lost by leaching, but large amounts can be present in the soil as insoluble salts which plants are unable to take up. The third of these vital elements, potash, gives disease resistance, encourages flowering and fruiting and is important in the development of storage roots and tubers. Though not as soluble as nitrogen, some loss through leaching does occur.

In theory it would be best to use a fertilizer compounded to meet the specific needs of each crop. But in a garden, where small amounts of a variety of crops are grown together, it is sensible to use a suitable general balanced fertilizer, such as Growmore or an organic equivalent like blood fish and bone, which provides the three major elements in suitable combination. A shortage or excess of any one of them can upset growth.

The fertilizer is added to the soil as a base dressing when it is prepared for sowing or planting, either raking or forking to mix it into the soil surface. A further amount may be an advantage for some long-standing crops or particularly greedy crops which can be applied as a top dressing between the plants and hoed into the surface. Take care to keep any inorganic fertilizer off the leaves lest it should scorch them.

Dry fertilizers have to dissolve to be of use to plants and should either be added to moist soil or, if rain is unlikely, the area should be watered after the fertilizer is applied. Many also require organic action in the soil to release the plant foods they contain, and moisture is needed by the organisms that bring about the changes.

Never forget that fertilizers are very rich in plant foods and that the recommended rates of application should not be increased. To do so may damage or kill the plants. Similarly fertilizers should always be spread as evenly as possible, not only to ensure all plants will receive a fair share, but to avoid the possibility of local over-dosing.

The speed at which fertilizers work depends on what they are made of. Those containing food that is readily assimilated gain a quick response. That of the remainder is dependent on the time taken to change the foods to a form plants can absorb.

Liquid Feeding

A faster response is gained by liquid feeding, where dissolved dilute fertilizer is applied in the water given to the plants rather than as a dry top dressing. Being dissolved, the fertilizer can be absorbed or acted upon immediately. Fastest of all is foliar feeding, where suitable feeds are sprayed over and absorbed through the leaves directly into the sap stream of the plants. Foliar feeding is particularly valuable where plants have received a check to growth, perhaps due to cold weather or pest attack, to get them growing swiftly again.

In the past liquid feeding was reserved for tomatoes, marrows, celery and other crops that needed a lot of moisture and food. The feed was usually prepared by soaking a bag of manure in a butt of water, occasionally prodding and stirring to dissolve its goodness. The resulting liquor was then diluted to a pale straw colour before being watered over the soil around chosen plants. Nowadays organic liquid feeds can be bought to serve the same purpose, as well as a range of easily dissolved, dry, inorganic products.

The introduction of modern hose-end dilutors, that automatically dilute special chemical feeds as the water issues from the end of the hose, makes it practicable to feed all the plants in a quite a large plot in this way, if you wish to do so.

WATERING

Many vegetables and all salad crops need to grow swiftly to maturity if they are to be of the best quality. Any check to their growth for lack of moisture can make them tougher and in some cases stringy. Such crops as lettuce and summer spinach run quickly to seed and runner beans fail to set pods if they suffer from drought.

Following winter rain, garden soil is usually at field capacity in early spring and holding as much moisture as it can, any surplus having drained down to the lower levels. As the season progresses, evaporation due to rising temperatures and wind dries the surface inch or two. Below that level it is plants that dry the soil by absorbing moisture. Where a seed bed is prepared in spring well away from encroaching roots of a hedge or trees and left empty until early summer, the soil below the surface remains very moist, whereas an identical area supporting plants can become very dry by that time if there has been little rain.

A certain amount of moisture is replaced by rain, but it is rare in Britain for summer rainfall to equal the amount of water extracted by plants. As the amount of soil water diminishes, the harder it is for plants to absorb it, and growth can suffer long before plants show severe stress by wilting. Watering to top up the moisture reserves should begin before this point is reached.

To be effective, watering must be done thoroughly, applying enough to moisten at least the top 30 cm (1 ft) of soil. Depending on the soil type and its capacity to hold moisture, this can take upwards of 22 l/m^2 (4 gal/sq yd) and in times of drought watering needs to be repeated weekly on light sandy soils and every 10–14 days on heavier ones with a greater moisture-holding capacity. Applying less than this can do more harm than good by encouraging the development of surface roots which are more likely to dry out.

Applying such large quantities of water needs to be done with care if the soil structure is not to be spoiled. The best method is to use a hose-pipe and sprinkler which can be left in position as long as is needed to supply the required amount. Check after 20 minutes by digging down to see how far the moisture has penetrated and assess how much longer the sprinkler is required to run. Once established this can be repeated each time the equipment is used.

Overwatering and watering before it is really needed are both wasteful since any surplus, together with the plant food dissolved in it, drains down beyond the reach of roots. On the other hand, do not be misled by summer showers when deciding whether or not to water. These often do little more than dampen the surface. It takes a pro-

Winter brassicas offer a wide variety of foliage textures and colours for several months of the year.

longed period of steady rain to remoisten soil after a dry spell.

On seed beds and newly planted areas where the soil surface is exposed, it is best to use a sprinkler that produces a fine misty spray. Large droplets pounding the surface could spoil the crumb structure and lead to panning — the formation of a surface crust as the soil dries. Such sprinklers cover a relatively small area and need to be moved quite frequently.

Once the soil is largely shielded by a canopy of foliage, sprinklers producing larger droplets with a longer throw can be used. Because they cover a larger area they are left in position longer and need fewer moves to cover a large plot.

Rotating pulse sprinklers are effective, but the circular watering patterns cannot be matched together without some overlap, which again is wasteful. Better is an oscillating type commonly sold for lawns which covers an oblong area. Where tall crops are grown raise the sprinkler on a box or other support to give it a clear throw.

For watering smaller areas, special hoses that allow the water to seep out along their length are available. These can be particularly useful for watering rows of runner beans, celery or other vegetables that need more moisture than ordinary crops.

Another method of watering marrows, tomatoes and other plants which are regularly liquid fed, is to use large pots or other containers with drainage holes and line them with plastic carrier bags, in the bases of which is a single pin hole. When the container is placed by a plant and filled with water or liquid feed, it slowly seeps out and penetrates deep into the soil without running over the surface. This is a particularly useful method for selected crops when the use of hose-pipes is banned.

It is a popular, but erroneous, belief that outdoor plants will be harmed if watered in sunshine, but where watering is done properly no harm will befall them as must be obvious by the daytime watering of crops done on farms and market gardens. It is certainly more efficient to water between late afternoon and mid morning since less moisture will be lost by evaporation, but if it is more convenient to water during the day, go ahead.

TRANSPLANTING

Although the majority of crops are started off from seed where they are to grow, some are transplanted from elsewhere in the plot to their growing quarters, others are raised under glass or bought and planted out. Any plant that is moved suffers some shock, often from loss of root, sometimes simply due to a sudden change of environment. Anything that can be done to reduce such stress will get them off to a better start.

The first step is to water seed beds the day before planting and ensure that the compost in containers is moist right through. The plants will then be fully charged with moisture and stand a better chance of survival.

Prepare the soil in the same way as for sowing by treading, adding fertilizer and raking. There is no need to prepare a fine surface tilth and it can be left much coarser. There will be no treading where a no-dig system is operated of course. Simply draw aside any surface litter and set the plants in place.

Almost all leafy brassicas, like cabbages and kales, are commonly raised from seed in a seed bed, then transplanted, to save space early in the season. Transplanting also encourages a more fibrous root system, while the plants are more stable due to being set deeper in the soil.

The traditional planting method is to pull the seedlings from the bed and plant them in holes made with the aid of a dibber, pressing the soil firmly about their roots with the heel of your boot. They are then watered in by pouring about half a pint of water around each one. Provided the seed bed is moist the pulled plants will have a small amount of roots and soil attached. Even so they will soon wilt and look sorry for themselves until they can make fresh roots, which they soon do.

Where only a few plants are to be dealt with and the seedlings were thinned to 5 cm (2 in) apart, it is possible to lift them individually with the aid of a trowel to keep a block of soil around their roots. The replanting holes must be made also with a trowel, the plants set a little deeper than before and the soil pressed firmly about them before being watered in. It takes longer to lift and plant seedlings in this manner, but the plants hardly wilt at all. Lettuce seedlings from early sowings can be moved in this manner.

Brassicas, lettuce, celery, tomatoes and other plants grown in pots or compartmented trays should also grow away with hardly a check if transplanted in a similar manner, setting each ball of roots and soil so it is just covered, pressing the soil firmly about it and then watering.

The roots of any seedlings in uncompartmented trays will have intermingled and, rather than tearing them apart, it is better to run a sharp knife along and across the tray between the rows. Then each can be lifted out with a fair share of roots and soil. Provided the tray was watered beforehand and the soil firmed about the plants' roots and watered, such seedlings should also grow away with hardly a check.

CHAPTER 8

Fruitful Surrounds

Fruiting trees and bushes form an ideal surround for an ornamental kitchen garden, most providing colour either when in flower or bearing ripe fruit that can be as effective as that of many of their purely ornamental relations. Trained flat to surrounding walls and fences or to post and wire supports, their formal shapes also add decoration for much of the year.

TRAINING

Any horizontal training wires required should be put in place before the fruits are planted. These can be run through vine eyes (Fig. 14), to hold them 10–15 cm (4–6 in) away from the face of walls and fences to allow air circulation behind the branches. Alternatively the horizontal wires can be run between stout wood or metal posts to create a free-standing support.

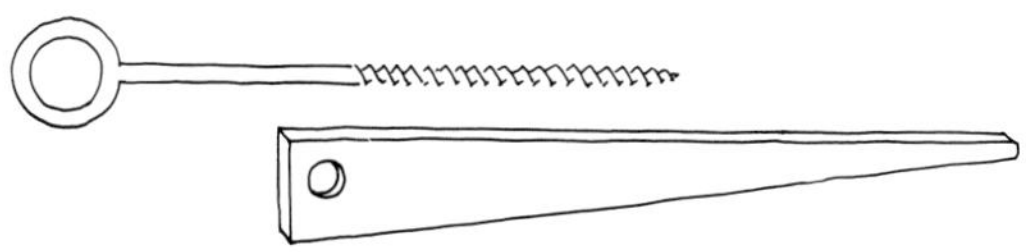

Fig. 14 *Use threaded or drive-in type vine eyes to hold horizontal training wires in place along the face of walls and fences.*

The number and position of wires will vary according to the type of fruit or the shape in which the trees are to be trained. For cane fruits like blackberries space the wires 30 cm (12 in) apart, starting 90 cm (3 ft) above soil level to the height required — usually 180 cm (6 ft). For cordon-trained trees and soft fruits, three wires at 60 cm (2 ft), 120 cm (4 ft) and 180 cm (6 ft) above ground will serve. Espaliers need wires 38–45 cm (15–18 in) apart for each tier of branches, the first usually being about 45 cm (18 in) above ground. For fan-trained trees and bushes the wires are better close spaced at 15 cm (6 in) apart.

The support space required depends on the fruit and type of training (Table 1, p.00).

Where blackberries, loganberries and similar hybrids are to be grown as fruiting pillars, put in stout upright posts reaching 2.1–2.4 m (7–8 ft) above ground.

PLANTING

The planting time for lifted trees and bushes runs from autumn through to early spring, while they are dormant, but the best time is autumn. Then the soil is still warm enough to encourage fresh root growth, even though the top growth of the plants is dormant, which will stand them in good stead should the following spring prove to be dry. Planting can be done at any time during this period while the soil is neither too wet and sticky to work nor frozen. Should the plants arrive when the soil is unsuitable for planting or at an inconvenient time, heel the plants in together in a bed to keep their roots moist. Dig a trench with one sloping side and place the plants close together along it leaning at an angle. Cover their roots with soil and tread in fairly firmly.

Lettuce offer a wide variety of colours and leaf shapes to give added contrast to vegetable plantings.

It is essential that the plants' roots should be moist. If they are dry on arrival, soak them in water for two hours beforehand to remoisten them. Then keep them covered with moist material or plastic sheeting until they are actually planted or heeled in. Immediately before planting, check the roots of each plant and trim off any broken or skinned root ends and shorten any odd long straggly root to the length of the others.

Dig the planting holes wide enough for the roots to be spread out fully and deep enough for the plants to be set as deeply as before (Fig. 15). There is usually a soil mark on the stem indicating the previous depth and this can be checked against a cane laid across the planting hole. It is essential that the bud union of any fruit tree, which can be seen as a lump on one side, should be well above soil level to prevent any possibility of the variety making roots and circumventing the restricting influence of the root stock.

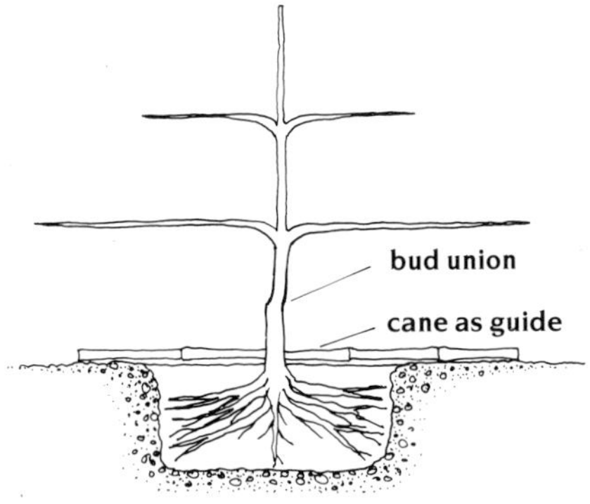

Fig. 15 *When planting a fruit tree excavate a hole wide enough for the roots to be spread out naturally and deep enough for the bud union to finish well above soil level, indicated by a cane laid across the hole.*

Work a handful or two of moist peat or composted bark in among the roots before refilling the hole with friable soil, a layer at a time, and treading it firmly with your foot. The soil must be made firm to give the plants stability as well as to encourage rooting and prevent it drying out quickly.

If you are planting a Ballerina apple or other pillar tree, prevent any possibility of damage to the roots by driving the supporting stake required into the base of the hole *before* putting in the tree. Alternatively use two stakes, linked by a cross piece to which the trunk can be tied. After planting loosen the surface 2.5 cm (1 in) of soil to destroy any foot marks, allow rain to penetrate easily and leave the area looking tidy.

Container-grown trees can be planted at any time of year, but because their roots cannot be spread out, they have to depend on the food and moisture they can gather from the original block of roots and soil until new roots develop into the surrounding soil.

Dig the planting hole deep enough for the root ball to be just covered with soil and wide enough to allow you to pack some moist peat around it. At the time of planting remove the container, of course, and loosen a few outer root tips. Ensure the plants never suffer from lack of moisture in the first year, especially if planted in spring or summer when the weather can be hot and dry.

Trees are usually planted upright. Cordons, however, should be planted at an angle of 45° with the scion uppermost; it helps to tie the supporting canes to the training wires first as a guide (Fig. 16). Where any tree is to be grown against a wall or

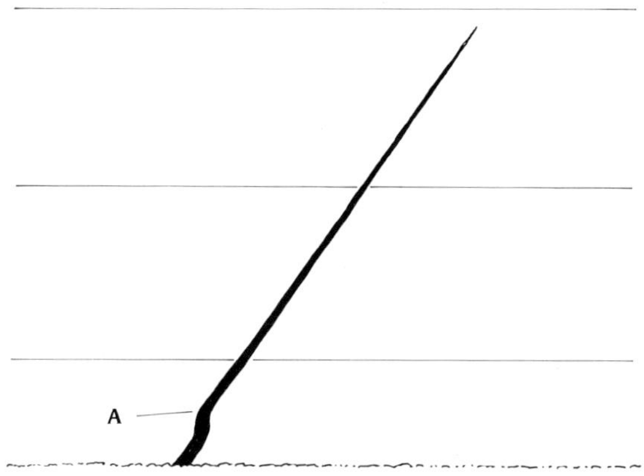

Fig. 16 *Cordon fruit trees should be set at an angle of 45° with the bud union (A) uppermost to prevent it splitting away when the stem is eventually lowered.*

fence, set its roots at least 30 cm (12 in) away from the base and lean it back slightly towards the training wires. This will allow space for the trunk to thicken and also keeps the roots away from what is often the driest area.

Although it may take a lot of self-discipline to do so, it does pay to remove all the blossom from fruit trees in the first spring following planting. This ensures the trees devote their entire energy to establishing a good root system and making growth that will lead to better crops in the future. Simply snip off the flowers with a pair of scissors.

PRUNING AND LATER TRAINING

Soft Fruit

Blackberries, loganberries and other hybrids make long new canes each year. They bear the best fruit on one-year-old canes, i.e. the canes that grew the summer before, so a healthy established plant will bear fruit on the older canes as the new ones are developing.

Immediately after planting in autumn or winter each plant should be cut back to a bud about 20 cm (8 in) above soil level. As the new canes develop in the first summer they can be tied to the training wires espalier fashion on either side of the plant, leaving the topmost wire vacant.

In the following and succeeding years the new canes should be trained upright in the centre of the plant as they develop and then along the top wire above the old ones. When the fruit is gathered the old canes are pruned out by cutting them off close to soil level and the new canes then released and tied in to replace them, leaving the top wire vacant again for the next crop of new canes. In late winter cut off any soft, unripe ends of the canes.

Where blackberries and similar fruits are trained as pillars, in the first year the new shoots are trained spirally around the posts. In after years the new shoots are tied in loosely to the support as they grow, to prevent damage. When the old canes are cut away after fruiting the new are trained in spirally to replace them. Any surplus growth above the post can be cut back to a suitable bud.

Red and white currants and gooseberries bear fruit on spurs that form along the old wood and are trained to form a permanent framework of branches. After planting cut back each of the shoots of cordons to remove about half the new growth and tie them to vertical canes. Remove any unwanted shoots from fan-trained bushes and cut back the new growth of the remainder to half length.

Afterwards pruning should be done in summer as well as winter. In summer, just as the currants are turning colour, cut back all new laterals (side shoots) to the fifth leaf, but leave the leaders (any shoot extending the length of an existing branch or needed to make additional branches on fans); these should be trained some 20 cm (8 in) apart untouched until winter. Summer pruning lets sun and air reach the ripening fruit, makes it easier to net the plants to keep off birds and encourages the development of fruit spurs along the branches. In winter remove about a quarter of the new growth from the leaders. Shorten all laterals again on red and white currants to leave only one or two buds at the base.

Laterals of gooseberries need slightly different winter treatment. Cut them back again to leave three buds on each.

Later when cordons have reached their required height and fan bushes the limit of the spread, the leaders can also be shortened to the fifth leaf in summer to restrict them.

Apples and Pears

After planting an espalier or cordon, tie the main shoots into position and shorten any side shoots to about three buds. Thereafter pruning is done mainly in summer.

In late summer, as the new growth ripens and becomes woody at the base, all vigorous laterals — those 23 cm (9 in) or more long —

Many herbs provide colour by way of flowers or foliage as well as adding flavour to dishes.

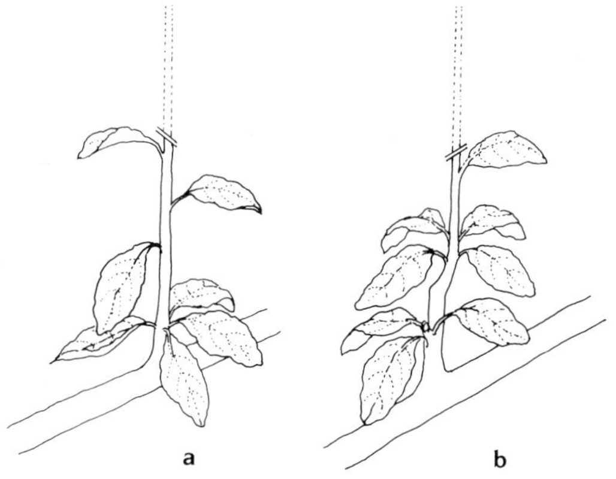

Fig. 17. *Summer prune apples and pears using the rule of 3 and 1. (a) Cut vigorous new side shoots arising directly from a branch back to the third leaf above the basal cluster. (b) Those springing from previously pruned shoots prune to the first leaf.*

should be cut back using the principle of 'three and one' (Fig. 17). All new shoots springing directly from the trunk or a branch should be cut back to the third leaf above the cluster around its base; new shoots arising from previously cut back shoots to the first leaf above the basal cluster.

Leaders should be left untouched at this time. The actual time of summer pruning will vary according to the season and area. Spread the work over several weeks to cut the shoots as each reaches the correct stage.

Summer pruning is important to control the vigour of the tree and to stimulate the development of fruit spurs. The removal of surplus growth in summer not only exposes the fruits to view, but also to sun and air, and apples, especially, develop a better colour.

In winter cut back the leading shoots to remove one quarter to one third of their growth — more where they lack vigour. Leave untouched any that have grown strongly. Only prune the leaders of cordons if the trees are not making enough laterals.

Where trees are trained against a wall or fence, any shoots growing towards the support should be removed completely each spring while they are still small.

To beginners it often seems a contradiction to cut away wood from weak shoots and leave strong ones untouched, but winter pruning stimulates growth and it is the weaker shoots that need to be stimulated the most. Remember the old gardener's saying, 'growth follows the knife'.

When cordons reach the top of their supports, they can be loosened and retied at a lower angle to give them more head room. Once the branches of espalier and fan trees reach the limit of their allocated space their leaders can be summer pruned also.

Ballerina trees need little pruning and detailed instructions are customarily provided when the trees are bought.

Espalier trees usually need to be trained to form extra tiers of branches. This is done by cutting back the central leader from the trunk in winter to a bud close to the next training wire. The top shoot that subsequently develops is trained vertically as it grows and a suitably placed shoot from either side at 45° as they develop. All other shoots are pinched out or removed entirely.

At the end of the season the angled shoots are bent down more or less horizontally to the training wire. These shoots must arise from below the training wire or they tend to split away from the trunk when bent down.

Fan-trained Plums

After planting, tie the ribs of the fan in position to canes tied in turn to the wires. Aim to make the sides of the fan first and fill the centre in later years. Shorten the ribs to some 60–75 cm (24–30 in) long when the buds break into growth the following spring.

Plums should never be pruned when dormant, since to do so encourages silver leaf disease. Each spring remove any shoots growing towards the support while they are small. Pinch back any growing directly away from the support to one leaf. Train in the extension growth of the branches as it develops, together with any lateral shoots needed to make new branches to fill in space. Remaining laterals should be thinned to about 10 cm (4 in) apart and their tips pinched out at the sixth leaf.

In late summer, or after the fruit is picked, prune these pinched back laterals to leave three leaves on each. This will encourage fruit spur development. Once the branches reach the limit of space available, pinch and prune their leaders in the same way as laterals.

THINNING FOR SIZE

Plums tend to over crop and produce a multitude of plums that are largely skin and stones. To have good-sized fruit in such seasons it is necessary to thin out the fruitlets to 7.5–10 cm (3–4 in) apart. Not only does this improve size and quality, but it ensures the tree does not exhaust itself producing seeds and then take a year off to regain strength before fruiting again. The number of fruitlets that need to be removed is often large, but efficient thinning does not necessarily mean a reduction in weight of crop, only that those retained are much fatter and juicier.

The thinning is best done in two stages, first in early summer to thin out the clusters, then again about a month later if necessary to the final distance required.

Pears and apples, too, may need to be thinned as the trees age to get good fruit size. Wait until after the natural fruit fall in early to mid summer, then thin out the clusters, first removing any malformed and small fruits. Leave dessert apples hanging about 10 cm (4 in) apart, culinary ones about twice that distance to get larger fruits.

CHAPTER 9

Problem Shooting

Inevitably problems of pests and diseases arise wherever plants are grown, and nowadays nothing divides kitchen gardeners more than the question of how to deal with them. Organic enthusiasts insist that no pesticides should be used at all and that reliance should be placed on good growing methods, natural predators and physical methods of control. At the other extreme there are gardeners who regularly use sprays on the 'just in case' principle to ward off troubles before they even appear.

Certainly one of the great advantages of growing your own food is that you know exactly what has happened to it. I, for one, do not want to eat anything that has been regularly sprayed with a variety of chemicals. On the other hand I do not want to lose the rewards of my labours — to find lettuces infested with greenfly, cauliflowers riddled with caterpillars, or have batches of brassica seedlings wiped out by flea beetles.

There are various cultural and physical ways to ward off and control many pests and diseases and these should always be the first line of defence. When this is breached I am quite prepared to dust seedlings with a little derris dust, or use an aphicide that kills only greenfly and not its predators. Following such a policy results in very few of the vegetables growing in my own garden being sprayed — some years none at all. It does mean, of course, that some may sustain a minor amount of pest damage, but provided this is acceptable it is possible to have a reasonable compromise. However, the amount of damage acceptable is less where vegetables are part of the ornamental scene. Sickly or dying plants and badly chewed and distorted foliage must be avoided if the area is to remain looking presentable.

First step in avoiding trouble is a matter of simple hygiene. Keep the plot tidy: do not leave plant refuse or other rubbish like brickbats and lengths of wood lying around that could harbour pests such as slugs and woodlice; keep down weeds that could act as hosts — flea beetles, for instance, thrive on shepherd's purse. Also never put diseased plant material on a compost heap — either destroy it by burning or dispose of it well away from the site.

Next give plants an adequate amount of space in which to develop. Overcrowding and weed infestation leads to a stagnant dank atmosphere where leaves do not dry off and diseases like white blister and ring spot of brassicas are encouraged.

Keep plants well fed and watered — it is the weaklings that are most prone to attack. Also take particular care not to overfeed with nitrogen, which leads to soft, sappy, disease-prone growth. Where there is a choice, and especially if problems have been experienced in the past, choose varieties noted for their resistance to it. For example, the parsnip variety 'Avonresister' is less likely to contract canker disease, and 'Avoncrisp' lettuces resist attacks of root aphids and mildew that can be troublesome in late summer.

Some pests and diseases are always with us, others come and go, being worse in some seasons than in others. Most damaging are

The silvery curry plant, **Helichrysum angustifolium** *scents the air with a mouthwatering aroma on warm days.*

those that attack under ground since you have no inkling they are there until it is too late. There are a handful, however, that every kitchen gardener should be able to recognize, together with the damage they cause, and know how to control.

PESTS

Slugs

One of the most common pests is the garden slug. It can do an enormous amount of damage, particularly to small seedlings in spring when the soil is moist. Later damage is confined mainly to leaves. They are most common on heavy ground that tends to lie wet. Their attacks can wipe out emerging seedlings so efficiently that the uninitiated may never realize that the seedlings appeared and blame poor germination. The pests are nocturnal, hiding away during the day, but a trip around the garden with a torch after dark can be a revealing experience!

Typical damage is rounded uneven holes in leaves and gnawed stems. The silvery slime trails made by the pests are normally visible.

Snails can also be troublesome, but usually close to hedges, rocky banks or old walls where there are holes for them to hide up in.

There are also underground slugs which attack roots and especially tubers. In bad attacks they can hollow away potatoes to leave little more than the outer skins. Such attacks tend to be worse in late summer and autumn, and where the ground tends to be heavily infested potatoes should be lifted as early as possible.

Control of the above-ground types is possible using a proprietary slug bait, trapping them in small containers containing a little beer, or gathering them up and destroying them after dark — not a job for the squeamish. They can also be trapped under half-grapefruit skins, cabbage leaves, pieces of wood or other things left on the soil for the slugs to congregate beneath. Such traps must be examined each day and any slugs harbouring there destroyed. Where infestations are large, baiting is the most effective method.

Underground slugs are much more difficult to contend with. They can be baited with slices of potato or carrots on skewers buried in the ground, but again the baits must be examined and 'de-slugged' regularly.

It is also possible to treat the ground with a product named 'Nobble' which kills slug eggs but, according to the makers, does not harm other soil inhabitants. It should be applied in autumn and spring to reduce the numbers of slugs.

One snag of manuring soil heavily or mulching it is that it can bring about an explosion in the slug population.

Flea Beetles

These are tiny yellow and black striped beetles that jump about. It is the silvery puncture marks made where they suck the sap from leaves that tend to be noticed rather than the pests themselves. They are most active where the soil is hot and dry and can be devastating.

Flea beetles will attack turnips and cauliflowers at any size, but with other brassicas it is the first kidney-shaped seed leaves that are the target and later growth is rarely affected. Uncontrolled they can wipe out complete sowings as they appear, particularly those made in late spring and summer. They can also kill off germinating rhubarb and severely check beetroot seedlings, though on these the puncture marks are not so easy to notice.

Though attacks of this pest can be severe if neglected, they are easily controlled simply by puffing a little derris dust along the seed rows as the seedlings push through. In a hot dry summer it may be necessary to treat turnips and cauliflowers a second time at a later stage also.

Cabbage Root Fly

This is a pernicious little fly that lays its eggs in the soil close to brassica plants. When they hatch, the whitish grubs burrow down

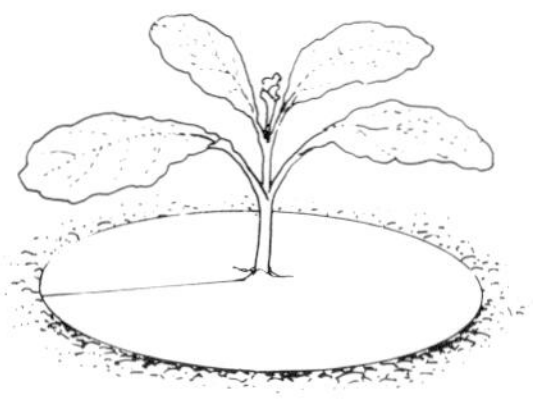

Fig. 18 *Brassica collars placed around the stems of seedlings at planting time help keep the grubs of cabbage root fly at bay without the need to use chemicals.*

and eat the roots but it may not be until the plants are half grown that they show distress and suddenly begin to wilt and then die.

All brassica plants should be protected from the moment they are planted out. This can be done by fitting a brassica collar (a small flat disc) around the stem of each plant to prevent the fly reaching the soil (Fig. 18), or dosing it with a soil insecticide, such as 'Bromophos', scattering a little of it around each plant and mixing it into the surface soil.

It is attacks to seedlings in a seed bed that are the worst problem. Once infested they are unlikely to recover. Protect the area by covering it with polypropylene fleece or treating the rows with a soil insecticide immediately after sowing. Alternatively plants can be raised under glass or bought in.

Carrot Root Fly

This is similar to cabbage root fly except that the grubs attack the roots of carrots and sometimes those of parsley, parsnip and related plants. The foliage of infested plants develops reddish tints. Again prevention is the best cure.

Always sow carrot seeds very thinly to avoid thinning out as far as possible. It is the smell that attracts the flies. Surrounding the rows with a 45 cm (18 in) high screen of clear plastic or glass seems to be effective at keeping this pest at bay. Also effective is growing the crop throughout the season under a layer of polypropylene fleece. It is wise to prepare the seed bed well beforehand and let the first flush of weeds germinate and be destroyed if using a complete covering. Alternatively the seed rows can be treated with a soil insecticide, though this needs to be repeated later to keep fresh hatchings of this pest at bay.

Aphids

Aphids, whether green, brown or black, are sure to appear at some stage. Where colonies appear on brassica leaves they can be squashed between finger and thumb. When on bean stems or tender foliage, or hidden in carrot foliage, this is not feasible and some sort of spray is the answer.

A modern aid similar to the Victorian soft soap sprays, such as 'Phostrogen Safers', is environmentally friendly, but being a contact spray it needs to be applied thoroughly and repeated as necessary. Derris, though often recommended, seems to have limited effect on aphids. Currently a better modern alternative is 'Rapid', which kills aphids only, not their predators or any other insects. However, it must not be used on marrows or related plants.

More difficult to deal with are root aphids which sometimes attack lettuce in summer. Where attacks regularly occur, grow a resistant variety. Otherwise drenching the soil with a suitable insecticide mixed to spray strength will control them.

Caterpillars

The caterpillar young of various butterflies and moths can attack a number of crops and fruits but are not often very damaging, except on brassicas. A serious infestation by caterpillars of cabbage white butterflies can strip whole plants to their leaf ribs if left to munch away happily. The green caterpillars of the cabbage moth, on the other hand, burrow into the hearts of plants and tend to be a worse menace.

Minor attacks can be controlled by hand picking and destroying the caterpillars. Caught when still tiny whole groups can be squashed. Even better is to crush the egg clusters if noticed — those of cabbage whites are bright yellow and usually laid on the undersides of leaves — to prevent trouble before it starts. Dusting or spraying with derris is very effective at controlling these pests. So, too, is spraying with a permethrin insecticide.

Brassica Whitefly

In recent years brassica whitefly has become much more common, seen as tiny white flies that rise in a cloud when the plants are disturbed. It is a pest that has developed resistance to many chemical insecticides and will no doubt do so with permethrin which has been quite effective so far. An alternative is soapy based 'Phostrogen Safers'. Whitefly passes through four stages in its life cycle and not all are susceptible to control by spraying which therefore needs to be done several times at 7–10 day intervals to have any hope of success.

There are usually at least some brassica plants in a well run kitchen garden at all times of year so there are always some host plants. If it becomes a serious pest, and your vegetable plot is fairly isolated, it may pay to make a break somewhere in the cycle to try and be rid of it, but there is not much point if there are infested brassicas in the garden next door.

Of course you could try the method suggested by one old gardener who, when asked how he controlled whitefly, said he waited for a windy day and then went and shook the plants so the pests blew away, but I don't think he was being serious!

Raspberry Beetle

Every kitchen gardener who grows cane fruits is likely to meet up with this pest in the form of tiny grubs in the fruits. The worst attacks usually occur on raspberries; it is easily controlled by spraying with derris as the first raspberries begin to turn pink. For other berried fruits the timing is different, so if it needs to be controlled on those, follow the maker's directions.

Apple Sawfly and Codling Moth

These are the adults of the grubs that burrow into apples. Those of apple sawfly attack early in the season and are gone by the time the fruit is ready to eat. Codling moth is the one to be found in early apples when they are eaten. If necessary, apple sawfly can be controlled, by spraying with a suitable insecticide when almost all the petals have fallen from the blossom in spring: codling moth by spraying in early summer and repeating according to instructions.

DISEASES

Club Root

This is a soil-borne disease of brassicas and, once a plot is infected, it is very difficult to control. The symptoms are sickly looking plants with large swollen roots. It can be spread by plants raised in infected soil, or in infected soil itself on tools and boots. It is most active in acid soil, which is why any lime needed should be applied to areas where brassicas are to be grown.

To minimize the chance of spreading the disease to an uninfected garden it is wise always to raise your own plants from seed, or buy them from a garden centre or nursery where the seedlings are grown in clean potting compost. Accepting gifts of plants from a friendly neighbour can lead unwittingly to disaster. Exercising the longest possible crop rotation helps prevent a build-up where there is an infection.

In theory the disease could eventually be starved out if the ground were kept clear of brassicas and all related crops and weeds, including turnip, radish, shepherd's purse and charlock, for long enough, but this would take many years.

There are various dips sold that will give temporary protection to newly planted seedlings, but these are not a cure. The only answer is to sterilize the soil in some way to be rid of it and considerable success has been claimed by some kitchen gardeners by

Pot marigolds and nasturtiums are easily raised from seed to add brilliant colour to a small bed of vegetables.

using 'Armillatox' that was originally developed to control honey fungus, another soil-borne disease that attacks trees and shrubs.

Onion White Rot

This is another soil-borne disease that attacks onions and other related crops, including shallots, leeks and garlic. The usual symptoms are yellowing leaves and poor growth and/or the development of fluffy white mould on the bulbs. Once infected the bulbs will not keep.

As with an infection of club root there used to be little one could do about it, apart from exercising the longest possible rotation or even giving up growing susceptible crops for many years. Now, however, the makers of 'Armillatox' suggest it can be used to control white rot.

Parsnip Canker

Yet another soil-borne trouble, this disease shows up as brown rotted areas mainly on the shoulders of the roots. Fortunately there are resistant varieties that can be grown, such as 'Avonresister' and 'White Gem'. Avoiding susceptible varieties and exercising a good rotation will prevent a serious build-up of the disease.

Potato Blight

This is an air-borne disease that appears in some areas without fail every year, though its virulence depends on the wetness of the season. It usually appears during early summer in the west, then sweeps across the country within a few weeks. The leaves and stems of potatoes turn brown, and spores washed into the soil also attack the tubers, which soon rot. It also attacks the fruits of the related tomato.

Potato blight can be controlled by spraying with a copper-based or other suitable fungicide. The spray must be applied as a protective covering preferably just before an attack is anticipated, but certainly as soon as the first sign of disease is noticed. Take care to wet both sides of the foliage and repeat according to the maker's directions to provide continuing protection.

When the haulm of potatoes is badly diseased, cut it down and remove it from the area to prevent spores washing into the soil. Tubers under a thick layer of soil are at less risk, so efficient earthing up of the crop helps protect them.

As potato tubers are picked up when harvesting, examine each one carefully for signs of greyish surface areas which could be infected. Keep these aside, for if an infected potato rots in store the disease quickly spreads by contact to others.

Apple and Pear Scab

These are two different diseases, but their effect is similar and control is the same. They are responsible for the brownish scabby patches on both fruit and leaves. Badly attacked fruits may crack and infections on young new growth may later lead to canker. Infected fruit will not keep for long. The pear variety 'William's Bon Chrétien' is very susceptible to pear scab.

Attacks are worse in areas that get plenty of summer rain. Spray with a suitable fungicide, starting as the trees break into growth in spring, and repeating according to need or directions.

Virus Diseases

Some crops are subject to virus diseases. These usually show up as stunted growth with smaller malformed or crinkled foliage, often with yellow spotting or mottling of the normal colour. Once a plant is infected there is no cure and it should be destroyed as soon as possible since it remains a source of infection for others.

Virus diseases can be seed-borne, spread by aphids moving from an infected plant to a healthy one, or by eelworms attacking the roots. They can also be spread by contact between one plant and another, as well as in the sap on hands and tools when working among the plants. The incidence of viruses is not normally great, but it pays to keep an eye out for unusual looking plants and 'if in doubt, have them out'.

Lettuce virus can be seed-borne, but any infected seedling usually stands out and is easily removed while young. In the case of potatoes, all the tubers from an infected plant will carry the disease. For this reason it is only safe to save seed potatoes from healthy plants and it is a wise precaution to replace all stocks with new certified seed tubers at least every third year.

In recent years attacks of cucumber mosaic virus on courgettes and marrows seem to have become more widespread. The yellow mottling is unmistakable. However, it does not appear on the old foliage formed before infection, but only on growth subsequently formed. It can spread along a row as the rough leaves and stems of plants scrape together in wind, but more often infection is transferred on a knife or secateurs used to harvest the fruits.

There are, of course, many other pests and diseases that crop up from time to time or may be endemic in local areas, but usually they are not particularly troublesome. Wireworms, for example, can be a nuisance during the first season or two where a kitchen garden is started from an area of meadow, lawn or a neglected weedy patch. This pest can be controlled by using a soil insecticide, but is unlikely to be troublesome afterwards if no grassy weeds are allowed to develop.

CHAPTER 10

Winter Stores

Some crops, like maincrop onions and potatoes, have to be stored after harvesting. Others such as beetroot can be enjoyed over a longer season if they too are lifted and kept safe, as well as clearing the ground for digging. Each needs to be treated differently. All stored produce must be undamaged and healthy if it is to keep.

The place where they are kept needs to be vermin-proof and, for most vegetables and fruit, cool but frost-free. These are not always the easiest conditions to find in a modern property where the only storage is usually a garage or shed, but by giving extra protection in hard weather, perhaps by an extra covering of newspapers or polystyrene, something can usually be contrived.

A good supply of boxes will be needed and wooden ones are almost a thing of the past. However, stout cardboard boxes, such as are used for packing sherry bottles, lined with polythene bags, serve very well. Nets are handy, also, for some crops and those used for marketing Brussels sprouts, carrots and oranges usually can be had for the asking from a friendly greengrocer.

POTATOES

The tubers must be kept cool, frost-free and dark. Select those for long-term storage carefully to avoid including any that are diseased. They can be contained in boxes or paper sacks, but metal dustbins lined thickly with newspaper work very well and solve the vermin problem. Allow air to get to them at first in case the potatoes should sweat, but be sure to keep them well covered in cold weather.

Examine the tubers within a month of storing and remove any that show signs of rotting. Thereafter they should keep soundly. Towards spring — if you have sufficient to last that long — they will begin to sprout, but the cooler they are the less trouble this will be. Once the shoots are about 2.5 cm (1 in) long, carefully turn out the potatoes, remove all the shoots, then return them to their containers. If the shoots are left to grow the tubers soon shrivel.

ONION FAMILY

Once the bulbs are fully ripened and dry, they can be cleaned of loose outer skin and soil, then either tied into ropes or stored loose in shallow trays or narrow nets. It is essential to allow a free circulation of air around them. Check them occasionally for any that show signs of rotting and remove them. Depending on the variety, thoroughness of ripening and storage conditions, the onions should easily keep until spring before they start into growth and spoil.

Shallots also can be stored in trays or nets when cleaned and dried. Yellow-skinned varieties store much longer than the red-skinned types which often show signs of regrowth early in the new year.

The best storage place for garlic is somewhere warm and dry. After the bulbs are cleaned, put aside any required for planting in a shed or garage. Tie the remainder in

The silver foliage of cardoons and related globe artichokes is elegant enough to warrant a place in a flower border.

bunches or strings and hang up close to the central heating pipes in a kitchen. Stored in this way they usually keep from one crop to the next without breaking into growth, whereas in a shed they can show signs of shoot growth as early as late winter.

MARROWS, SQUASHES AND PUMPKINS

Marrows and the related pumpkins and squashes should be gathered when mature, at which stage they will have made a hard outer coat. They can be stored on a layer of straw and covered with the same material in an outhouse or hung up in nets. Alternatively cleaned of soil they can be stored in any convenient place indoors. Some are so colourful that they make interesting indoor decorations.

CARROTS

Carrots can be lifted when mature, the tops cut off close to their crowns then stored in boxes of peat, sand or even sifted reasonably dry soil (Fig. 19). First spread a layer of the material over the base of the box, then space out a layer of roots close together, but not touching, and cover them over. Continue putting in and covering layers until the box is full. The roots can be drawn on as required until they finally break into growth in spring.

Depending on the variety and soil conditions, some carrots can be left in the ground over winter. Summer varieties may split when the autumn rains come and rot if the ground is too wet over winter. Granted reasonably drained soil 'Berlicum' and 'Autumn King Vita Longa' are reliable types to leave in the ground, but it is worth storing a few in a box to provide a supply should the ground freeze solid and prevent lifting of those outdoors.

Fig. 19 *Mature roots of beetroot and carrots can be stored in layers in boxes of sand or peat for winter use. Arrange the roots close together without touching.*

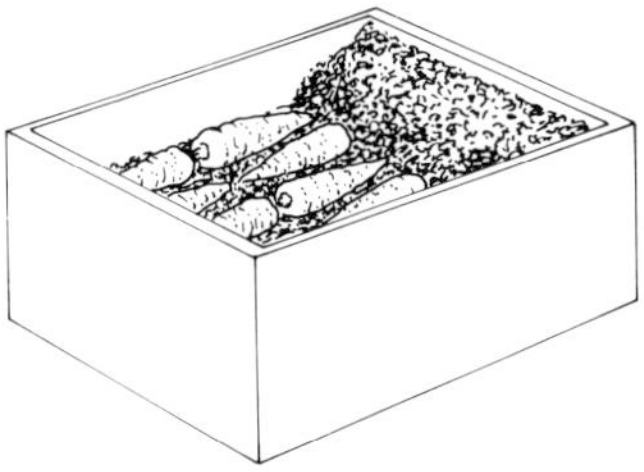

BEETROOT

Beetroot can be stored similarly to carrots except that their foliage is best wrung off, not cut off, and the thin tap root below the round root left undamaged. They must be lifted with special care. If the roots are damaged they bleed and lose quality.

OTHER ROOT VEGETABLES

Roots of winter turnips and winter radish can be left outdoors at first, but are liable to split if frosted. Where winters tend to be harsh it is worth lifting and storing those remaining in early winter. Treat exactly the same as for carrots.

Chicory roots grown for forcing can be stored in similar manner. After lifting cut off their tops about 2.5 cm (1 in) above their crowns and shorten the parsnip-like roots to about 20 cm (8 in) long.

CELERIAC

It is better also to lift and store remaining celeriac roots in late autumn lest they be spoiled. Lift carefully with the aid of a fork, then strip away all the old leaves to leave just the youngest ones surrounding the central shoot. Bury the roots in a box of moist peat, sand or soil, leaving their shoots exposed.

APPLES

Ideally apples need a dark, airy, cool but frost-free place that is humid enough to prevent them shrivelling but most home gardeners can offer little better than space in a shed or garage. Only sound, disease-free apples complete with stalks are likely to keep for long and particular care should be taken when picking not to bruise them or puncture their skins.

Keep the varieties apart, as far as possible, or the ethylene gas given off by earlier ripening fruits may trigger premature ripening of late varieties. Fruit can also be tainted by strong smells or fumes, such as is given off by paint, creosote, fertilizer and other garden sundries and resinous wood.

The fruits can be stored on slatted trays, or in shallow boxes with holes along the sides to allow for ventilation. Wrapping the fruits individually in tissue or newspaper keeps them clean and helps prevent the spread of rots from one to another, but makes it difficult to inspect them.

Alternatively apples can be kept in clean, clear polythene bags large enough to hold about 3 kg (6½ lb), which prevents shrivelling (Fig. 20). Punch a few holes in the bags to allow some ventilation and either fold over or loosely tie the ends. Check the fruits regularly and remove any that show signs of rotting.

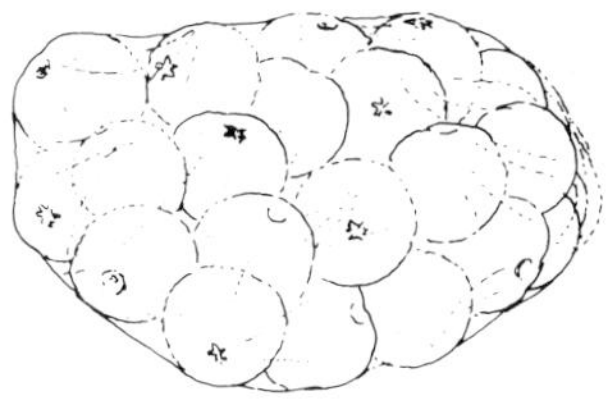

Fig. 20 *Sound apples are less likely to shrivel if stored in polythene bags with a few holes poked in them to provide some ventilation.*

PEARS

Sound pears need similar storage conditions to apples, but should not be wrapped or kept in polythene bags. They are best arrayed in single layers on wide shelves or in trays where they can be examined easily for signs of ripening — usually indicated by a slight change from green to more yellowish colour — at which stage they should be taken into a warm room for a few days to finish ripening.

CHAPTER 11

Weed Control

Every kitchen gardener soon learns that if you disturb soil to any depth it will produce a new crop of weeds. These largely spring from weed seeds buried in the soil being brought to within about 2.5 cm (1 in) of the surface where they then germinate; seed beds prepared to obtain good germination from crops are just as encouraging to weeds. Other weed seeds may be blown in by wind, or spread by birds and animals.

Weeds have to be controlled because they compete with crops for food and moisture and smother low-growing plants completely. Some also harbour the same pests and diseases which attack vegetables and could act as host plants providing a link between one susceptible crop and the next. A weedy plot also looks very untidy and this will not do where the aim is an ornamental kitchen garden.

The amount and type of weeds you have to contend with at first depend on the history of the ground. If the kitchen garden has been created from pasture land there will be comparatively few, but if it is made in an old garden or neglected arable area the soil could be packed with weed seeds and be infested with a lot of perennial weeds.

INITIAL CLEARANCE

Ordinary grasses can be skimmed off the surface and buried in the trench during the initial digging where they will rot down. Perennial weeds, such as docks, dandelions, buttercups and nettles, can be forked out at the same time, taking care to remove every scrap of root. If the ground is infested with couch grass or pernicious ground elder, however, it will save a lot of heartache if they are first killed off with a total herbicide. One containing glyphosate is very effective if applied thoroughly at the recommended strength when the weeds have sufficient foliage to absorb a lethal dose. It is slow acting, but does not poison the soil. An alternative is to use ammonium sulphamate, sold under the name of 'Root-Out'. This is poisonous to plants at first, but is soon converted to a nitrogenous fertilizer to stimulate growth.

Having dug and cleared the ground of existing weeds, aim to keep it as weed-free as possible. This may call for some effort at first but will bring its rewards. Never let weeds flower if you can avoid it. To allow them to seed is to store up trouble for the future. There is much truth in the old gardeners' saying, 'One year's seeding — seven years' weeding'. As time goes by weed problems will gradually lessen as the supply of weed seeds in the soil is reduced.

FIRST FLUSH

Where possible, it is helpful to rake and prepare as much ground as possible early in the season. The first flush of weeds that inevitably develops can then be killed off ahead of sowing or planting to reduce their numbers later. Although there will always be some late developers, the majority of weed seeds in the surface germination layer will have grown and been destroyed.

One of the advantages of no-dig methods of cultivation is that provided weeds are not

Courgettes and other vegetables can be grown in pots and other containers beside a path.

allowed to seed over the surface, there are fewer germinating weeds to contend with, because the soil is not regularly disturbed to any great depth.

The customary method of keeping the soil clear of weeds is by hoeing. This should begin shortly after sowing or planting and continued as required throughout the life of the crop. As soon as vegetable seedlings push through the soil use a Dutch hoe between the rows, working as close to the seedlings as possible without endangering them. Skimming just below the surface the blade severs or uproots the weed seedlings, most of which then die. Hoeing also breaks any surface crust that may have formed to allow free aeration.

It should be followed up by a second hoeing within ten days, provided the soil is dry enough to allow it. This will dispose of most germinating weeds. Thereafter hoe as conditions seem to warrant, but do aim to kill weeds while they are tiny. Once you let them develop in size many, including annual meadow grass, bird's eye, chickweed and groundsel, tend to survive and reroot into the ground.

After a third hoeing, therefore, it pays to take a plastic bucket and pull up and remove the few survivors. Also any growing close to plants which were missed when hoeing. From that time very few more weeds should appear.

When properly spaced the maturing crops themselves also help control weeds by covering the ground with a canopy of foliage that effectively smothers weeds germinating underneath. Provided you do not allow any survivors to develop before then the ground can stay remarkably clean.

ORGANIC MULCHES

Mulching the soil with a layer of organic matter also smothers germinating weeds. By preventing surface evaporation mulches are also claimed to conserve moisture. This is true, but I doubt if the amount of moisture saved really amounts to much. What is more important is that by keeping the soil surface covered and moist, plants root into and make full use of the surface inch of fertile top soil that is otherwise largely useless to them either by reason of dryness or hoeing.

Apart from organic mulches, such as rotted manure, garden compost, peat or bark products, all of which look presentable and can eventually be worked into the soil to improve it, almost any material can be used for mulching from straw, grass clippings and newspapers to old carpet. None is sightly, however, and any which begin to rot may result in a temporary loss of soil nitrogen.

PLASTIC SHEETING

Black plastic sheeting, preferably microperforated to allow penetration of moisture, is also a weed-defying mulch. It can be difficult to handle, however, since the edges must be clamped into the soil to hold it in position and it tends to balloon up in windy weather if not held down with stones or even a little earth at intervals over the surface. Neither is it handsome to look at, though it is eventually largely hidden by foliage. It is effective however where a lot of cabbages, onions or potatoes are grown.

After the ground is prepared for planting it is covered with sheeting, the edges being inserted into slits made with a spade. Cabbages, other brassicas and onions sets can be planted through the plastic by punching holes with a dibber. Potatoes can be planted first and then covered. When their shoots begin to push up the plastic, it can be cut to allow them through. A few weeds may appear through the holes which need to be winkled out, but that is all. Using this method, potatoes do not need to be earthed up since the plastic blocks out light that would turn them green.

Harvesting of potatoes is greatly simplified. When they are ready, simply strip away

Paved areas can be utilized in a small garden to produce crops of vegetables and herbs in pots.

Fig. 21 *Potatoes grown through a mulch of black plastic sheeting do not need to be earthed up – a particular advantage where they are grown in small beds.*

the plastic and gather the tubers, most of which are at or just below the surface (Fig. 21). Onions can be left until their tops shrivel before the plastic is stripped off and the crop lifted. Although the bulbs are denied sun, they still develop a good colour.

There is one major disadvantage to using mulches of any kind. If the garden is infested with slugs they cause more damage. A dry surface in summer does deter their movement.

WEEDOL

Hoeing cannot be done efficiently when the soil is too wet. Also the number of weeds surviving is greater if rain follows hoeing. If weeds get out of hand in a wet season, it is possible to control them by applying the herbicide called Weedol. This kills all green growth but does not taint the soil. It can be used among growing crops provided scrupulous care is taken to keep it off the plants.

WEED DISPOSAL

All seedling weeds and large annual weeds that have not yet run to seed can go on a compost heap to rot down. The remainder should be destroyed, or disposed of away from the plot.

SECTION II

Vegetable Crop Guide

ARTICHOKE, GLOBE

Plant: spring
Harvest: summer

These are perennial plants with large, handsome leaves and are decorative enough to warrant a place in a flower border. The part eaten is the inner flesh of the large flower buds before they open. If left they develop into large, purple, thistle-like flowers.

Plants can be raised from seed and a sowing made in late spring provides heads to cut in late summer or early autumn. Select the best plants to increase and scrap the rest. When obtainable, plants of French-named varieties are superior, but tend to be less hardy and their crowns may need winter protection.

Plant 90–120 cm (3–4 ft) apart in a sunny, spot in well manured ground. Mulch the soil about them with manure or garden compost each spring, augmented with fertilizer if necessary. Plants can be kept for 4–5 years; then replace.

Cut buds with few scales when the first layer begin to open back: those with many scales when two or three layers have opened. Remove each with 15 cm (6 in) of stem.

Remove dead stems and foliage in autumn and fill any holes in the ground with friable soil. Cover crowns for protection if necessary.

Propagate new plants by removing suckers (basal shoots springing from the crown) when about 15 cm (6 in) high in spring from old plants. Ensure each has a piece of the old crown and some roots attached. Press the soil firm about them and water in well.

ARTICHOKE, JERUSALEM

Plant: early spring
Harvest: autumn and winter, as required

Jerusalem artichokes are grown for their tubers. The plants grow over 180 cm (6 ft) tall and need careful siting to avoid shading other plants. The tubers have an unusual smoky flavour when cooked, but are nutty tasting when raw. The common type produces about a bucketful of large knobbly tubers per plant: the variety 'Fuseau' a smaller crop of carrot-shaped tubers.

Plant in a sunny spot. Set the tubers 38 cm (15 in) apart and 10–15 cm (4–6 in) deep, leaving 90 cm (3 ft) between rows.

In windy sites support the stems with wires run between posts driven in at intervals along the row. When the growth dies in autumn, cut down the stems to 30 cm (12 in) high.

The tubers do not keep well out of the soil and discolour in light. Lift as required, taking care to remove all tubers. Any missed will grow again the following spring.

ASPARAGUS PEA

Sow: late spring
Harvest: summer

This oddity is more vetch than pea, but can be grown in almost any soil in a sunny place. The plants are not hardy and should not be sown too early. Their brick-red flowers make an unusual display.

Sow the seeds in pairs 45 cm (18 in) apart, leaving 60 cm (24 in) between rows. Later thin to single seedlings. Growth tends to be floppy and needs supporting with twiggy sticks or strings on either side of the row. The unusual winged pods are normally picked when about 2.5 cm (1 in) long.

BEAN, BROAD

Sow: late winter, spring and late autumn
Harvest: late spring and summer

Broad beans are hardy and are best picked and eaten before they become 'black-eyed' and floury. The beans soon age, so make several sowings to provide a succession.

Beans and peas obtain nitrogen from bacteria which live in small nodules on their roots. They do not need nitrogen,

Ornamental in blossom and when carrying fruit, espalier trees repay the attention needed to train them.

therefore, but appreciate plenty of phosphates which encourage the bacteria. The bacteria occur naturally in Britain, but in some countries it may be necessary to 'inoculate' the soil to introduce them.

Sow the large seeds 20 cm (8 in) apart in two rows spaced 25 cm (10 in). Leave 60–90 cm (2–3 ft) between double rows. Set the seeds 5 cm (2 in) deep, either two at each station, or singly with a few extras between the rows to transplant later to fill any gaps. Later, support tall varieties with wires strung between canes to enclose the row. Choose a dwarf variety for exposed sites.

Plants from spring sowings are usually attacked by blackfly shortly after they begin to flower. Pinching out the top 7.5–10 cm (3–4 in) of the stems can help ward off attacks, but must not be done too early.

In mild areas the hardy variety 'Aquadulce Claudia' can be sown in late autumn or early winter to provide an early crop which is less likely to attract blackfly. The site must be sunny, reasonably sheltered and well drained.

When the crop is cleared, cut down the stems and remove them to a compost heap. The roots can be dug into the ground where they provide a source of nitrogen.

I particularly favour 'Jubilee Hysor', which produces eight or nine beans per pod without wasted space. Also 'Feligreen' that is only half as tall as the standard varieties, has shorter pods but plenty of them. It is ideal for an exposed plot, as are the dwarf types like 'The Sutton'. The beans of 'Red Epicure' are a bronze colour and many claim them to have a superior flavour.

BEAN, FRENCH

Sow: spring to early summer
Harvest: summer

Dwarf French beans provide pickings before the runner beans, and their flowers set pods freely. Haricot beans also belong to this group. Climbing varieties can be sown and supported similarly to runner beans. The plants are tender and cannot survive being frozen. Sow in late spring so the seedlings emerge when danger of frost has passed.

The dwarf varieties can be sown several times at about three-week intervals to provide a succession, and if cloches are available to cover them later, a final sowing can be made at mid summer to provide autumn pickings.

Set the seeds 10 cm (4 in) apart along 5 cm (2 in) deep furrows. Leave 35 cm (18 in) between the rows. Later support the plants with string or wire run along either side of the row. Begin picking as soon as the pods are full grown, but before they become stringy. Use two hands to gather the pods by detaching the stalks cleanly from the plants.

Leave haricot beans until the pods turn yellow, then pull up the plants and hang up in loose bundles in a sunny position to finish drying. In a wet season they should be dried under cover. Once the pods are brittle remove the seeds and spread them out on paper to finish drying before storing in jars.

'The Prince' and 'Masterpiece' are two old and very reliable flat-podded dwarf varieties. Of the modern ones my choice is 'Delinel': a heavy cropper, it holds its pods up high and is easy to pick. For colour and flavour the yellow-podded 'Mont d'Or' and purple-podded 'Purple Queen' are excellent.

For drying, 'Dutch Brown' has proved its worth over the years. Dual-purpose 'Cheverbel', with lime-green seeds, can be picked fresh or dried for seeds.

BEAN, RUNNER

Sow: late spring to early summer
Harvest: mid summer to early autumn

Runner beans are one of the most valuable summer crops for gardeners in Britain, because they bear over a long season to produce a large return from a small area. They are 'long-day' plants, however, and will not flower when grown too close to the equator where days and nights are nearer the same length.

The plants need a sunny, reasonably sheltered position and a soil enriched with plenty of organic matter. Lacking sufficient sun they produce luxuriant growth but few or no flowers, and if they become dry at the roots the flowers will fail to set pods.

Although most varieties are climbing, there are dwarf types that develop as low bushes. They bear a little earlier and seem to have far less trouble in setting pods, but their season is shorter. They are particularly useful for exposed sites.

The traditional method is to grow runner beans in a double row running north to south, with plants spaced 23–30 cm (9–12 in) apart, leaving 30–38 cm (12–15 in) between the two rows.

Dwarf varieties are grown in single rows allowing 23 cm (9 in) between plants and 60 cm (24 in) between rows.

In small gardens it is more convenient to grow the climbers in a circle 120–150 cm (4–5 ft) across. This creates less of a shade problem.

Climbing varieties need long canes or poles to twine about. Thrust them into the ground along either side of the double row at an angle so they lean inwards and cross about 30 cm (12 in) below their tops. Others are then placed horizontally along the crotches so formed and the whole structure tied securely.

Where the beans are grown in a circle the supports are leant into the centre and tied securely at the top to form a 'wigwam'. An alternative is the use of proprietary metal bean supports that hold strings in a circle.

Runner beans are tender and killed by frost. Sowing in late spring should be timed to ensure seedling emergence occurs after danger of frost is over. Set the large seeds 5 cm (2 in) deep where each plant is required, plus a few spares to transplant to fill any gaps. Alternatively sow two seeds about 2.5 cm (1 in) apart at each station and later remove the weaker seedling if two appear. Where an early crop is wanted, make an earlier sowing under cloches or raise seedlings under glass to plant out.

Keep the plants moist and begin harvesting when the first pods are fully grown but before the seeds swell large. It is important to pick two or three times weekly, removing all pods that are ready, if the plants are to keep on bearing.

'Enorma' is very reliable and bears longer pods than most. 'Painted Lady' has very attractive red and white flowers, but its pods become stringy more quickly.

For a dwarf variety, try 'Pickwick'. It produces an excellent crop of shortish pods and is very colourful during its flowering period.

BEETROOT

Sow: early spring to mid summer
Harvest: summer and autumn

Beetroot is one of the easier crops to produce, is relatively quick growing and can be closely spaced to save room. The 'seeds' are actually capsules containing several seeds, although those of 'monogerm' varieties produce only one seedling and are an advantage at thinning out time. The capsules also contain a germination inhibitor which must be leached out before the seeds will grow.

Sow small batches every three or four weeks up to mid summer to maintain a succession of fresh roots. Use a non-bolting variety for early sowings. Sow a batch towards the end of spring to provide roots to store for winter.

Sow the seeds thinly along shallow drills spaced 30 cm (12 in) apart, and thin to 10 cm (4 in). Flood the drills immediately before sowing unless the soil is quite moist to ensure good germination. If you have adopted a form of bed culture, sow across the bed in rows 10 cm (4 in) apart, dropping the seeds at the same distance.

Begin harvesting the earliest sowings when they are about golf-ball size. Leave those for storing until they are mature. At all times avoid damaging the roots, otherwise they bleed and lose quality.

The quickest maturing variety for early sowing is 'Replata', making a flattish globe. 'Monodet', and 'Boltardy' are also reliably non-bolting and make larger roots. For a maincrop one of the 'Detroit Globe' selections should offer the best quality. For extra size choose 'Cylindra'. 'Burpee Golden' offers golden-fleshed roots, while 'Albina Vereduna' is white fleshed and very sweet tasting.

BROCCOLI, SPROUTING

Sow: late spring
Plant: summer
Harvest: winter and spring

Sprouting broccoli can be white or purple. It was an important crop for cottage gardeners, providing pickings for several weeks in spring before spring-sown crops were ready. Nowadays there are strains that come into season at any time between Christmas and late spring. For autumn there is Italian, or green, sprouting broccoli (see calabrese).

Raise the seedlings in a seed bed and plant out 60–75 cm (24–30 in) apart each way. The plants may be killed in severe winters and need shelter from north and east winds.

Harvesting begins when the flower shoots appear. Snap them off taking a short piece of soft stem and leaves with the cluster of purple or white buds at the tip. More shoots develop from the leaf joints of the portion remaining than can be gathered in turn. Seed packets may be labelled just white or

purple sprouting broccoli or as early or late. There is also 'Christmas Purple Sprouting Broccoli', which is much earlier than the others if the winter is mild and open.

BRUSSELS SPROUTS

Sow: early spring
Plant: late spring
Harvest: autumn and winter

Brussels sprouts are the most popular of the winter brassicas grown in Britain, and because they can be picked over many weeks, they are one of the most useful winter crops. Raise plants in a seed bed to plant out.

Allow the plants plenty of space. Lack of air circulation can easily lead to ailments like leaf spot and mildew. A spacing of 90 cm (3 ft) apart each way was customary and is still the best. A few well grown plants will give many pounds of sprouts.

This crop is subject to all the common brassica ailments and if the soil of the planting site is acid it should be limed. Where the site is exposed, stake the plants to keep them upright.

Begin picking the sprouts when they are large enough to use. The crop can be speeded up to some extent by cutting out the tops of the plants to concentrate their energy into the developing buttons. The tops make excellent greens to eat, but if taken too early the crop will be curtailed.

Always pick from the bottom up, clearing the stem as you go. Any which have opened up should be removed as well. Plants still in the ground in spring eventually go to seed. Their flowering shoots can be gathered, cooked and eaten like sprouting broccoli.

Brussels sprouts are classified as early, mid season and late. For a good autumn and winter crop most gardeners grow a mid season and late variety.

'Peer Gynt' is one of the oldest mid season F_1 hybrids, but still excellent for garden production. It is ready from mid autumn and provides picking for about three months. 'Fortress,' 'Widgeon' or 'Wellington' are reliable to provide pickings after mid winter.

CABBAGE AND SAVOY

Sow: early spring, late spring, mid summer
Harvest: most of year

Cabbages and crinkle-leaved savoys can provide heads to cut almost the year round. They are divided into four groups — early summer, late summer and autumn, winter and finally spring — according to when they are ready to harvest. Not many kitchen gardeners bother with more than an early sowing of summer cabbages since there are plenty of other crops mid summer onwards, but during the colder months and in spring they are the mainstay of the green vegetables.

The plants are best grown in an open, sunny position. Manured ground is ideal, though not essential, and it should be only slightly acid if at all.

Raise the seedlings in a seed bed, or under glass, to plant out. Spacing depends on variety and varies according to size. Ideally the plants should just touch when approaching maturity, so that weeds are smothered.

Sow summer and red cabbages in early to mid spring, the sowing date determining when the heads are likely to be ready for cutting. Sow autumn and winter cabbages in late spring. Harvesting time depends on the varieties chosen. Similarly the date when spring cabbages are ready depends on variety and all are sown in late summer.

It is imperative to control cabbage root fly where seedlings are raised outdoors. For later sowings, particularly those of spring cabbages, also keep down flea beetles.

When the plants are set out, the soil should be made really firm about their roots. Again it is important to ward off cabbage root fly. For the rest of the summer the main pests are aphids and caterpillars.

Begin cutting from a batch of plants when the heads are reasonably firm. If you wait until all are drum-hard, some are likely to spoil.

Spring cabbages are overwintered as quite small plants and complete their growth cycle in the spring. They are not suitable for growing in really cold areas unless the rows are covered with cloches in winter.

If the seedlings are planted at half the normal distance apart in the rows, alternate plants can be cut early as leafy greens, leaving the remainder to mature. Apply nitrogenous fertilizer between the rows in late winter to prod them into growth and make them more tender.

One of the best early summer cabbages 'Marner Allfruh'

Low-growing step-over trees make a fruitful and productive edging yet cast little shade.

makes tight round heads fit to cut before being fully mature. Sown under glass in winter and planted out under cloches it can provide sizeable heads for cutting in late spring. Even quicker growing, but smaller, is 'Hispi' with pointed heads. 'Derby Day' is another good round cabbage for raising under glass or outdoors for summer cutting.

'Wiam' is an excellent cabbage for late summer since its round heads can stand for a couple of months or more without spoiling. Maturing a little later, the pointed 'Winnigstadt' is an old variety that still shows its worth.

For autumn and early winter 'Christmas Drumhead' — don't be fooled by the name as it is ready about two months before Christmas in Britain — followed by 'January King' will see you through to the festivities. 'Celtic' is another excellent choice for late autumn.

'January King Hardy Late Stock 3' can be relied on to provide purple-tinged heads from mid winter onwards, as can the F_1 hybrid 'Tundra' and the true savoys 'Ormskirk Late' and 'Alexander's No.1'.

For spring cutting 'Pixie' is very early maturing with small pointed heads. It can be followed by the roundheaded 'Spring Hero'.

Red cabbages are ready in late summer or early autumn. 'Ruby Ball', 'Norma' and 'Red Drumhead' are neat growing, compact and produce superb round heads. All bring a welcome variety of colour to a kitchen garden.

CALABRESE

Sow: late spring or summer
Plant: summer
Harvest: late summer and autumn

Italian calabrese is a green form of sprouting broccoli. Most varieties produce a sizeable central head like a small cauliflower, followed by smaller side shoots. This is another cut-and-come-again crop so useful for a small garden, but those with the largest central heads usually produce the smallest crop of following shoots.

The normal recommended time for sowing is early to late spring, but the early plants begin to bear when other summer vegetables are in full spate, and calabrese must be picked as soon as ready or it soon runs to flower. Unless required for freezing it can pay to delay sowing so the crop is produced in autumn.

Like other brassicas an open sunny position is needed. The crop is best where the soil is rich and the plants get plenty of moisture.

The central head should be cut when fully developed, but before it begins to open up. The following side shoots are gathered in a similar way to sprouting broccoli, which needs to be done 2–3 times weekly.

The F_1 hybrids, such as 'Corvet' and 'Topstar', give the most even crop of large heads. Where the aim is for the longest harvest of fresh shoots an ordinary variety like 'El Centro' or 'Calabrese Green Sprouting' is more rewarding.

CARROT

Sow: early spring to mid summer
Harvest: summer to spring

Tasty carrots are appreciated by almost everyone, whether cooked or raw, and bring appetizing colour to any dish. They are an easy and rewarding crop to produce provided carrot root fly is controlled.

Carrots do best in the lighter soils where their roots are less constricted, but good crops can be grown on heavier soil provided the ground is not allowed to become excessively dry. Where the ground is well drained in winter, mature roots can be left *in situ* and dug as required. If not they are better lifted and stored in boxes of sand or peat.

If the seeds are sown very thinly along the drills all the roots can be left to develop. This saves the fiddly job of thinning and lessens the chance of attracting carrot root fly, but inevitably leads to some roots being smaller than others, Alternatively the seedlings can be thinned out when 2.5 cm (1 in) high. Allow 2.5 cm (1 in) between the seedlings for early summer crops: 5 cm (2 in) for large roots to store. Space the rows 30 cm (12 in) apart.

Where an intensive bed system is adopted the seed can be sown broadcast and the seedlings thinned to about 5 cm (2 in) apart. Alternatively sow in close-spaced rows across the beds.

Harvesting of the earliest sowing begins as soon as the roots are large enough to use – a little more than pencil thickness — in late spring. Leave maincrop carrots for storing until they are fully grown.

Successional sowings can be made every three weeks to maintain a regular supply of very young roots. Alternatively make two major sowings — one in early spring to provide summer roots, another in late spring for autumn and winter use.

Carrots do well under cloches and can be sown in late winter to get extra-early pullings.

Carrot varieties vary and should be chosen to match their use. For early sowings under cloches or outdoors choose one like 'Amsterdam Forcing' that will quickly give small, usable roots. For summer use the cylindrical 'Nantes Tip Top' or stump-rooted 'Chantery Red Cored' make larger roots. Both can also be lifted and stored when mature. For winter use the cylindrical 'Berlicum' and stump-rooted 'Autumn King Vita Longa' are very reliable and are unlikely to split if left in the ground.

CAULIFLOWER, SUMMER

Sow: spring
Harvest: summer and autumn

Summer cauliflowers are one of the trickiest brassica crops to produce unless you have suitable soil. They need ample food and plenty of moisture to produce large, white heads and must grow swiftly to maturity. Should their growth be seriously checked by adverse weather, drought or pests, they tend to form tiny heads about 5 cm (2 in) across.

Ideal soil is a deep rich loam, though given care and attention they can do well anywhere except on very light hungry ground or where the soil is just a thin layer overlying chalk. The more heavily manured the area the better, and a dressing of balanced fertilizer is needed as well. Raise the plants like cabbages in a seed bed.

To spread the season some varieties can be raised in autumn and over wintered in a cold frame. Others can be raised early under glass, but they must be carefully hardened off and acclimatized to outdoor conditions before they are planted out. A cold snap following planting, or too cold a soil could check them.

At each stage take steps to ward off cabbage root fly and to keep down flea beetles, which continue to attack cauliflowers after the seedling stage.

Throughout the growing season water plants whenever the soil begins to dry out. Once the crop is about half grown give the plants a top dressing of nitrogenous fertilizer to keep them growing.

The heads are ready for cutting when the inner leaves open back fully to expose the white curd. Examine them daily and snap a leaf over any partially exposed head to shade it until ready for cutting.

One of the snags of summer cauliflowers is that the plants tend to head up together. It is better therefore to grow a small amount of a number of different varieties to spread the season. Select them and the growing method according to the time of year you need to cut them. Sown outdoors in spring most will be ready in late summer or early autumn. One of the easiest to produce is 'Dok Elgon', a strong grower with plenty of leaves. Now a number of F_1 hybrids are being introduced which, being stronger growing, may be more forgiving of less than ideal conditions.

Akin to the summer cauliflowers is the autumn giant group. These head up in late autumn and early winter. Because of their longer growing season they are far less inclined to bolt.

CAULIFLOWER, WINTER

Sow: late spring
Harvest: late winter to summer

Winter cauliflowers are a different race to the summer varieties. They are hardy, take 9–12 months to mature and do not tend to bolt. They do, however, need protection from cold winds and may be killed completely by a harsh winter.

They need to develop into large, sturdy plants before the onset of winter. Manured ground and a base dressing of fertilizer before planting will satisfy their needs, though a boost of nitrogenous fertilizer in late winter can improve size and quality.

Varieties that head up in winter are only suitable for growing in very mild areas and those that mature from early spring onwards are best for most gardens. Reliable winter cauliflowers include Walcheren Winter types such as 'Armado April' (early spring) and 'Markanta' (mid spring). Also the English winter favourites like 'St George' (early spring) and 'Late Queen' (late spring).

CELERIAC

Sow: early spring under glass
Plant: late spring
Harvest: autumn and winter

This is a kind of root celery, that forms a large basal knob at ground level. It can be used raw in salads or in cooked dishes. The leaves can also be used for flavouring. The plants are grown on level ground, not in trenches.

This crop appreciates well manured, rich soil and plenty of warmth and moisture. Sow the seed in a cold frame or greenhouse in spring. Once large enough the seedlings should be pricked out into trays and grown on until planted out when danger of frost has passed. Alternatively buy plants in late spring.

Set the plants 30 cm (12 in) apart, leaving 45 cm (18 in) between rows, or 30 cm (12 in) apart each way in a bed. Keep them watered in dry periods. Occasionally check for and remove any suckers growing from their bases, together with some of the oldest leaves, to encourage growth.

Begin lifting plants as required for use in early autumn. Lift and store the remainder in early winter.

'Prague Giant' is one of the easiest to grow to a large size, but discolours when cut. Some modern selections such as 'Tellus' remain white. 'Monarch' is a fine new introduction.

CELERY, MAINCROP

Sow: early spring under glass
Plant: late spring
Harvest: autumn and winter

Maincrop, or trench, celery is a challenge to any kitchen gardener. It needs a deep, rich soil and ample moisture if the sticks are to be crisp and tender. Any check to its growth will cause the stalks to become stringy. It is not a suitable crop for heavy clay or sandy ground.

Plants are raised under glass in spring, pricked out into boxes and planted outdoors in late spring. The planting site should be prepared in winter by double digging a strip and working plenty of organic manure into the subsoil, then excavating a trench 38 cm (15 in) wide for a single row, 45 cm (18 in) wide for a double row, and about 23 cm (9 in) deep. Spread and level the soil from the trench as a flat-topped ridge on either side.

Set out the plants 23 cm (9 in) apart and water them in well. Thereafter they must be kept well supplied with moisture and they benefit from liquid feeding.

Maincrop celery needs to be earthed up to blanch the leaf stalks, which is done in stages, beginning in late summer when the plants are some 30 cm (12 in) high. Remove any suckers from the plants' bases, then loosely tie the stalks together with a length of soft string or raffia. The soil should be moist and friable and a 10 cm (4 in) layer can be heaped around the plants. More is added at intervals until the plants stop growing, at which stage the final earthing up in early autumn should cover the stalks to just below the leaves. The final mound should be steep sided and patted smooth with a spade.

At each stage prevent the soil from falling into the plant centres. It helps to tie strips of corrugated cardboard or newspaper around the plants as collars. Use a narrow one first, then add others as required so each overlaps the one below.

Maincrop celery has some frost resistance, but will not withstand severe weather. Protect the tops when hard frost is likely.

Lift plants as required from autumn on until the crop is finished, beginning at one end of the row and replacing the soil to keep remaining plants well covered.

White and pink or red varieties are available, the coloured ones being the hardiest. White celery is best used by Christmas.

CELERY, SELF-BLANCHING

Sow: early spring under glass
Plant: late spring
Harvest: summer and early autumn

Self-blanching celery is grown on the flat and is easier to produce, but is not hardy and should be used before autumn frosts arrive. It needs just as much food and water if the sticks are to be tender. Plants are raised in the same way as maincrop celery and planted out about 23 cm (9 in) apart in a frame for an early harvest, or in a block in the open so the plants blanch each other. Surrounding the sides of the block with boards to shade the plants at the edge improves their quality.

Keep the plants watered and well fed. The plants will tend to bolt if their growth is checked. Begin lifting them in summer as

Those cane fruits with long, lax canes, like this loganberry, are easily trained over an archway.

soon as they are large enough to warrant it. Fill any gaps with straw or crumpled newspaper to block out light.

'Lathom Self-Blanching' has bolt resistance and produces sticks of high quality. 'Celebrity' is also bolt-resistant, produces longer and heavier sticks, but takes longer to mature.

CHICORY, FORCING

Sow: mid summer
Lift: autumn
Force: late autumn and winter

Any kitchen gardener prepared to force chicory will have chicons vastly superior to any that can be bought. Ageing and exposure to light cause the chicons to become bitter, whereas fresh blanched chicory is crisp and nutty flavoured.

This is an easy crop which is grown in two stages — first outdoors to produce the roots, then forcing these in warmth and complete darkness during winter to produce the blanched chicons. Roots about 4 cm (1½ in) wide at the top are ideal. Sow the seed in late spring or early summer in rows 30 cm (12 in) apart and thin the seedlings to 15 cm (6 in).

Lift the roots in autumn. Cut back the foliage to within 2.5 cm (1 in) of the crowns and shorten the roots to some 20 cm (8 in) long. Store them in a box of sand or peat until required for forcing.

Force the roots in batches to provide a succession from late autumn onwards. Set them upright in boxes or pots filled with moist soil or old potting compost deep enough to leave the crowns just exposed. The containers can be housed anywhere convenient where gentle warmth and darkness can be maintained. Alternatively the roots can be planted in the soil bed of a greenhouse or conservatory and watered well in. The old 'Witloof' varieties need to be covered with 17.5 cm (7 in) of dry sifted soil or sand to keep the chicons tightly closed, which also keeps them dark. Some modern varieties need only be covered with upturned boxes or pots, remembering that the covering must be completely light proof.

Harvest the chicons when about 15 cm (6 in) high, cutting them off just level with the root. Those under a covering of soil or sand are usually ready when the surface cracks and begins to lift. A temperature of 10–16°C (50–60°F) is ample for forcing.

For many years only 'Witloof' was offered. Now there are different strains including an F_1 hybrid, 'Witloof Zoom'. Choose 'Normato' to grow without a soil covering.

CHICORY, HEADING

Sow: summer
Harvest: autumn and winter

Heading chicory is an excellent salad crop, with a slightly bitter tang. It is particularly good late in the year when the summer lettuce have come to an end, and can often be cut throughout the winter. It is very easy to grow, does well in any average soil and stands for months.

Sow the seed in drills 45 cm (18 in) apart during summer and thin to 30 cm (12 in) in the rows. It should be possible to grow them 30 cm (12 in) apart under a bed system. The cos-lettuce-like heads can be cut at any time once large enough.

Radicchio is a red-leaved form of chicory that makes rather smaller heads. It can survive early frosts, but is generally better used in autumn. The roots can also be forced if required. Its leaves are crisper than ordinary heading chicory and their colour is very welcome in the kitchen garden.

One of the oldest varieties, 'Sugar Loaf', is very hardy and reliable, as is the newer 'Crystal Head'. Radicchio has only recently received much attention in this country but it is worth growing either 'Rossa de Verona' or 'Palla Rossa' to cheer up those autumn and early winter salads.

CHINESE CABBAGE AND PAK CHOI

Sow: summer
Harvest: late summer and autumn

Chinese cabbage is a fast-growing crop that can be used as a salad or cooked. If you have the right conditions it is easy to grow, but it will bolt to seed at the slightest provocation.

This crop needs rich soil, warmth and plenty of moisture. Sowing the seeds outdoors before early summer causes it to bolt, and many gardeners find it safer to wait until mid summer.

Choose a warm, sheltered bed and sow the seeds very thinly along rows spaced 30 cm (12 in) apart. Thin out the seedlings to the same distance. Keep the plants well watered at all times. Harvesting begins about 70–80 days after sowing and, when ready, the heads will not stand for long.

Pak choi is another oriental

vegetable that is related to, but much more reliable than Chinese cabbage. Instead of making a heart, it produces a rosette of dark green leaves, each having a very crisp and juicy stalk. It makes a pleasant addition to a salad or to a mixture of stir-fried vegetables and can be grown in the same way.

Every year new Chinese cabbage varieties seem to replace the old in seed lists. 'Kasumi' is barrel-shaped, shows some bolt resistance and is well worth trying. Pak choi is usually just listed under its own name, but there is one called 'Joy Choi' that is delightful to eat.

CORN SALAD

Sow: summer and autumn
Harvest: summer to spring

Few kitchen gardeners bother to grow corn salad, but it is very useful where space is limited. It grows in any reasonable soil, is quick and can be sown late in the season when the ground is cleared of summer crops. You are unlikely to want it when lettuce is available, but in autumn and spring it earns its keep.

Sow along rows spaced 10 cm (4 in) apart and thin to the same distance. Harvest either by plucking individual leaves from each plant or cut complete heads of leaves. The heaviest crop comes with spring growth as the plants are preparing to flower.

The plants are best covered with cloches in winter to keep them clean. Under cloches growth continues longer and late sowings can provide a useful harvest in winter.

Varieties include 'English', 'Broad Leaved English', 'Large Leaved Italian' and others similarly named. Don't worry which it is — just buy yourself a large packet and sow at intervals from late summer.

COURGETTE, MARROW, SQUASH AND PUMPKIN

Sow: late spring or early summer
Harvest: summer and early autumn

The traditional vegetable marrow is a British vegetable not widely grown elsewhere. Courgettes (zucchini) and squashes are established favourites over most of the warmer areas of the world and the less commonly grown ones need more warmth than marrows and generally do better if sown a little later. All, however, are well worth growing, particularly the winter squashes with their more solid texture and better flavour. All appreciate humus-rich soil, full sun and plenty of moisture. Where space is limited choose those that have bushy growth.

Sow the seeds, two or three together on edge and 2.5 cm (1 in) apart and deep where each plant is required, thinning to one after germination. Spacing depends on variety, but bush types can be grown 60 cm (24 in) apart. If growing several rows arrange them in pairs 60 cm (24 in) apart, leaving 90 cm (36 in) between the double rows. If you have a frame or greenhouse it is better to sow the seeds in small pots and plant out the seedlings, preferably under cloches at first, in early summer.

Pinch out the growing tips of trailing types when they have made six leaves and train the resulting side shoots in the direction required.

Gather courgettes, summer squashes and baby marrows while they are young to ensure the plants continue flowering and producing more. Leave winter squashes and marrows for storing until they are mature and tough skinned in late summer before harvesting.

There are many different courgette varieties. I prefer those with dark green fruits like 'Ambassador' and 'Zucchini', but a golden-fruited one like 'Gold Rush' makes a bold splash of colour. For young striped marrows 'Zebra Cross' is among the very earliest, but one of the standard varieties like 'Green Bush' or 'White Bush' gives larger fruits for storing.

Squashes come in many shapes and sizes. The patty-pan 'Custard White' and 'Custard Yellow', with scalloped edges are uncommon summer varieties. Best for flavour are the winter squashes, such as green and white 'Table Dainty' and dark green 'Table Ace', both small fruited. 'Vegetable Spaghetti' with cream, 20 cm (8 in) long, oval fruits, and the much larger 'Golden Hubbard Squash' are all good eating and worth growing if you can spare the space.

Of the pumpkins, 'Jackpot' produces spherical fruits about 25 cm (10 in) across; the fruits of 'Mammoth' are large, but the easiest to grow to a huge size is 'Atlantic Giant'.

CUCUMBER AND GHERKIN

Sow or plant: early summer
Harvest: summer and early autumn

Cucumbers and gherkins need a warmer soil than marrows to do really well and except in mild areas outdoor sowing is best delayed until early summer. For an early crop they can be raised in pots under glass and planted out later.

They need rich soil, full sun and plenty of moisture. Space plants 60–75 cm (24–30 in) apart. Sow two or three seeds where a plant is required and thin to one later. Pinch out the tips of trailing varieties at the sixth leaf and train subsequent side shoots to fill available space — even over a tripod of canes or a chain link fence.

Harvest cucumbers as soon as they are large enough to eat. Keeping them cut encourages continuous cropping. Remove the first few gherkins that form, and wait for a picking numerous enough to pickle.

'King of the Ridge' is still a very popular outdoor cucumber. However, the recently introduced space-saving bush varieties like 'Bush Crop' and 'Bush Champion' are likely to take over from the trailing varieties. Gherkins are more difficult to track down. Grow 'Conda' if you can find it, or 'Venlo Pickling'.

Tayberries can be trained to slim trellis panels or poles as a centrepiece to a formal design.

ENDIVE

Sow: mid summer onwards
Harvest: autumn and early winter

Endive, a close relative of chicory, is a salad crop. It is too bitter to eat unless its growth is blanched, so there are two stages to its production. Few people want it when lettuce is available.

Growth needs to be swift so give endive a humus-rich soil in an open position and plenty of moisture. Late crops, especially, will not survive in cold, soggy soil.

There are two types: curly leaved, which is used for early sowings, and the hardier smooth leaved that can stand into the New Year in northern climes if protected with cloches. Depending on variety they can be grown 23–30 cm (9–12 in) apart, but remember you will have to cover them later and allow space for this.

Begin blanching the plants when they are almost fully grown, about 12 weeks after sowing, by covering a few at a time. Choose a day when the foliage is dry and tie the leaves loosely together with soft string or wool about 10 cm (4 in) from the top. Cover each plant with a larger flower pot and block the drainage hole. Alternatively a handyman could make a long, light-tight box of suitable dimensions to cover several plants together, the best way if you are using bed culture. Blanching takes some three to five weeks, depending on the time of year. Once blanched the plants will not keep for long.

The broad-leaved 'Batavian Green' and 'Green Curled' are the two most common varieties. 'Golda' is an improved broad-leaved type, 'Coquette' a more uniform curled one.

FENNEL, FLORENCE

Sow: mid summer
Harvest: autumn

Although looking similar to the herb fennel, this is an annual which swells up its leaf bases to form a 'bulb' at ground level. Very young plants can be chopped into salads to add flavour. When full grown and cooked, the bulbs have a pleasant, very mild taste. The plants bolt to seed if sown too early.

Sow in an open position in rows 30 cm (12 in) apart and ensure the plants never lack moisture. Thin out early to about 20 cm (8 in) apart. It is customary to earth up the bulbs a month before harvesting to blanch them, but this seems unnecessary if they are fairly well shaded by other crops and are harvested while still young. There is always a danger that they will run to seed if left too long. Bolting was a serious drawback with old varieties, but two I have found reliably non-bolting are 'Sirio' and 'Zefa Fino'.

GARLIC

Plant: autumn to spring
Harvest: late summer

This is one of the easiest crops to produce, granted a reasonably fertile, well-drained soil and an open, sunny site. The bulbs are broken into individual cloves that are planted 2.5–5 cm (1–2 in) deep and 15 cm (6 in) apart in rows spaced at 30 cm (1 ft). In beds set them 15 cm (6 in) apart each way. Best planting time is mid autumn, but it can be done any time until spring.

When shoots appear keep the soil weeded and water in dry spells. Lift and dry the bulbs when the foliage yellows. After drying and cleaning store the bulbs in a *warm*, dry place to keep them dormant.

You can start off with a bulb bought in a shop, but because different strains are grown and imported from different parts of the world, it is worth buying a stock of a locally grown strain if possible to start with. 'Long Keeper', for example, is one that does well in Britain.

KALE

Sow: spring
Harvest: autumn to spring

Kales belong to the cabbage tribe and are often spurned by kitchen gardeners, yet they offer pickings of fresh leaves and shoots for salading or cooking over many months of the year. The crop per plant is never large, but they are good stand-bys. Those offering the longest harvest period can be most valuable where space is limited.

Plants are normally raised in a seed bed and planted out later. They must be protected from cabbage root fly. Normal spacing is 60 cm (24 in) apart. Tall-growing plants should be staked in exposed gardens.

Harvesting, depending on variety and season, is a matter of picking young foliage and/or shoots.

'Tall Green Curled' and its dwarf counterpart produce good pickings from autumn until they eventually run to seed in spring. 'Spurt' is even better. A single early spring sowing can provide pickings (first from the thinnings) for about 10 months and is superior in flavour.

'Pentland Brig' provides masses of tender shoots from late winter and is well-flavoured. Granted space, 'Cottager's' and 'Thousandhead' are worth growing for their spring shoots.

KOHL RABI

Sow: spring to mid summer
Harvest: summer and autumn

This is a strange-looking brassica that produces a bulbous stem above ground from which the leaves protrude. It is quite quick growing and does well in ordinary soil in an open site, but is subject to the usual brassica pests and diseases. It can be used raw or cooked and provides early pickings when used small — about 4 cm (1½ in) across.

Plants can be raised in a seed bed and planted out, or sown direct in rows. Normal spacing is 23–30 cm (9–12 in). It will put up with drier conditions than turnips and does better on light soils.

Begin harvesting as soon as large enough to eat. The plants will eventually reach the size of a tennis ball, but the lower half of the 'bulb' becomes very fibrous if allowed to get too old.

'White Vienna' and the colourful 'Purple Vienna' have been available for many years. F_1 hybrids are now available and 'Rowel' seems a definite improvement.

LEEK

Sow: spring
Plant: late spring and summer
Harvest: autumn to spring

Leeks are easy to grow and one of the most reliable winter crops. The winter varieties are unharmed by the harshest weather and pigeons never touch them. They do not seem to be troubled by pests, and though they may get a touch of rust disease in some seasons, it is never too bad. If you particularly want leeks in late summer, raise the plants under glass or buy them.

Since the plants are set out in 15 cm (6 in) deep dibber holes, the deeper the soil the better, but they are not unduly fussy. Raise the plants in a bed, sowing the seeds thinly along drills spaced 23 cm (9 in) apart. Plant them out when about 20 cm (8 in) high.

Lift the seedlings, cut their roots back to within 8 mm (¼ in) of their bases and shorten the leaves a little. Drop them into the dibber holes and fill the holes with water. If they are planted with their leaves pointing along the rows the gaps between rows remain clear, making it easier to hoe. Space them 15–23 cm (6–9 in) apart. Allow 30 cm (12 in) between the rows, and 45 cm (18 in) after every third or fourth row as a path. Under bed culture set them 20 cm (8 in) apart each way.

Begin harvesting as required in autumn, or as soon as large enough to eat. They will continue to put on growth in mild periods and again for a few weeks in spring before they finally run to seed.

'Musselburgh' is one of the

hardiest and very reliable, with thick, sturdy stems. 'Autumn Mammoth Argenta' has a longer shaft, bulks up quickly and is well flavoured.

LETTUCE

Sow: early spring to late summer
Harvest: late spring to autumn

Lettuce is the most important and popular salad crop grown outdoors and certainly one of the easiest. Like other salads it enjoys humus rich soil and ample moisture. The quicker the plants mature, the more tender they will be. Once mature, lettuce soon run to seed and it is essential to make fresh sowings at about two-week intervals through the season if you aim to have a continuous supply.

Sow very thinly along rows spaced 30 cm (1 ft) apart. Thin out the seedlings to 15–30 cm (6–12 in) apart, depending on variety. Early in the year it pays to thin to half the final distance at first. Alternate plants can then be taken when their leaves touch to give an early harvest. Where grown intensively in beds, distance between rows can equal the plant spacing.

Seedlings from early sowings can be transplanted. Those from later sowings will bolt if moved, as they will if their growth is seriously checked in any way, particularly by drought.

The lettuce season can be extended by making an early sowing in late winter under cloches and another in late summer that can be covered with cloches in early autumn. In mild areas it is also possible to make an autumn sowing of a very hardy variety, such as 'Valdor', 'Arctic King' or the cos lettuce 'Winter Density', to provide an early crop in spring. A warm, sheltered, well drained site is needed.

Lettuces come in many different forms and may be soft or crisp, large or small, plain green, tinged with red, or completely red. There are non-heading types, too, that provide pickings of leaves for many weeks and are useful standbys should the succession of hearted lettuce break down. Broadly the cos and crisp-leaved varieties take longer to mature than the soft-leaved ones, and the bigger the variety the longer it will also take to grow. Choose one that you enjoy eating and which is of suitable size.

Of the soft, 'butter-headed' varieties, 'Tom Thumb' is very small and compact, quick growing and can be spaced 15 cm (6 in) apart. 'Dolly' is much larger and produces superb heads. 'Avondefiance' is resistant to lettuce root aphid, mildew and bolting and is especially useful for summer sowings where these problems are common. 'Continuity', an old variety with red-tinged leaves, is bolt-resistant and worth growing on light soils.

Among the crisp-leaved Iceberg types, 'Lakeland' and 'Avoncrisp' are both resistant to mildew and and root aphids, the former being one of the fastest maturing of this group.

One of the best cos lettuces is 'Little Gem'. Rich green, small and compact with well formed hearts it is quick growing, crisp and delicious. 'Angela' is similar, but easier to break apart into individual leaves. Both can be grown about 15 cm (6 in) apart and I prefer these to any other lettuces. Another fine, small cos type of startling colour is 'Apache'. The dark purple-brown colouring of its outer leaves contrasts starkly with others.

'Salad Bowl' and its red counterpart are two popular non-hearting lettuce. They provide pickings for many weeks before finally running to seed. Red-tingled 'Lollo Rossa' is a more refined type with better flavour and crisper, more crinkled leaves.

ONION

Sow: spring and late summer
Plant sets: spring and early autumn
Harvest: mid summer or early autumn

Onions are a very satisfying crop to produce, but are hardly worth bothering with where space is limited. Growing them from seed can be tricky if you do not have the right soil, but good results can be had even on heavy ground by planting onion sets (small immature bulbs).

This crop needs an open, sunny situation and a firm seed bed. Sow the maincrop in spring, scattering the seeds very thinly along drills spaced 30 cm (12 in) apart and later thin seedlings to 10–15 cm (4–6 in). Surplus seedlings can be transplanted or eaten as spring onions.

Plant sets by spacing them the same distance apart along 2.5 cm (1 in) deep drills, then carefully draw the soil back over them and tamp it down with the head of a rake. The spacing for seedlings and sets can be reduced to 15 cm (6 in) apart each way when grown intensively in beds.

As maturity approaches the tops of the plants topple over. Gently tuck them between the rows to expose the bulbs to sun. Once the foliage withers, lift the bulbs and spread them on wire-mesh trays held off the soil with bricks or logs to finish drying and ripening. Alternatively spread them out in an airy shed or greenhouse if the weather is unsettled. Once fully dry they can be stored away. Well-ripened onions should keep until spring.

To close the gap between the end of one crop and the next it is possible to grow extra early ripening onions by sowing special varieties in late summer, or planting sets in early autumn. The bulbs from these ripen about two months earlier and can be used 'green' before that.

To grow from seed 'Bedfordshire Champion' is an old and reliable variety but is outclassed by modern hybrids such as 'Hygro'. 'Albion' is a white onion, almost spherical in shape, with quite a pungent flavour. 'Southport Red Globe' is a reliable red variety to grow from seed — as yet there are no reliable red onion sets.

With one exception there does not seem a lot of difference between the onion sets available. Choose one with the shape and flavour that suits you. The exception is 'Giant Fen Globe' which is heat-treated and has by far the greatest bolt resistance.

Most varieties suitable for sowing in late summer are of Japanese origin and 'Senshyu Semi Globe Yellow' is one of the best. 'Puma' is a new British variety. 'Unwins First Early' is the onion set for autumn planting.

ONION, SPRING

Sow: early spring to early summer and late summer
Harvest: late spring to autumn

The name spring onion is rather a misnomer, since it is only over-wintered plants that are usually harvestable in spring. Normal spring sowings are ready in summer and autumn. Make sowings at roughly three-week intervals to maintain a summer supply of young plants, and a final late sowing in late summer for the following spring.

Sow thinly along the rows and leave them unthinned. Normal row spacing is 30 cm (12 in), but this can easily be reduced by half when grown intensively in beds.

Begin pulling the plants as soon as they are large enough to eat, first loosening them with a fork.

'White Lisbon' is the traditional variety and still the best flavoured. For a late summer sowing to over-winter choose 'Winter White Bunching' or 'White Lisbon Winter Hardy'.

PARSLEY, HAMBURG

Sow: spring
Harvest: autumn and winter

Sown early and well thinned out Hamburg parsley makes a large parsnip-like root with a somewhat celery-like flavour. It makes a pleasant change to the common winter vegetables and can be used raw in salads as well as cooked. Young leaves can also be used for flavouring.

Hamburg parsley does well in ordinary well-drained soil and should not be given fresh manure. It can be attacked by carrot root fly, but otherwise is usually easy to grow.

Sow the seeds very thinly in rows spaced 30 cm (12 in) apart and thin to about 20 cm (8 in). Germination is slow so it pays to scatter a little radish seed along the rows to mark them. Grown in beds the plants can be spaced 23 cm (9 in) apart. Begin lifting roots for use as required in autumn.

This vegetable is usually just listed under its name, but one or two specific varieties, like 'Omega', are now appearing in catalogues.

PARSNIP

Sow: spring
Harvest: autumn to spring

This is another crop not to bother with if you are short of space, unless you love them as I do. Given reasonable soil and an open site, parsnips are usually trouble free to grow. The area should have been manured for a previous crop. Do not dig in fresh manure but add a dressing of fertilizer before sowing.

Scatter the papery seeds thinly along rows 38 cm (15 in) apart and later thin the seedlings to 15–23 cm (6–9 in). Alternatively sow two or three seeds where each plant is wanted along the row and single the groups later. Where grown intensively in a bed, space rows and plants 23 cm (9 in)

Good use is made of a dwarf wall by planting cordon-trained gooseberries and growing cucumbers up canes beside it.

apart. Parsnips are slow to germinate so it pays to scatter a little radish seed along the drills as well to mark them quickly.

Begin harvesting in autumn, lifting the roots as required and clearing along the rows.

'White Gem' is a good all-round variety that has some resistance to canker disease. 'Avonresister' has greater resistance, but its roots tend to be much smaller unless well spaced out.

PEA, GARDEN

Sow: spring to summer and late autumn
Harvest: late spring to autumn

You need a lot of space to produce peas in succession throughout the season, also a deep moisture-retentive soil for the summer crops. Most people grow only a row or two to provide pickings before the runner beans begin to crop. Peas sown in autumn will crop in late spring. Spring sowings crop in summer. A final sowing of a dwarf variety at mid summer can be picked in autumn.

Peas do best in a liberally manured soil and an open sunny site. Like beans the plants get nitrogen from bacteria on their roots. Too much nitrogen in the ground encourages excessive growth.

Sow the seeds 5 cm (2 in) apart along two 2.5–4 cm (1–1½ in) drills spaced 15 cm (6 in) apart to allow a hoe to be run between them. Space the double rows at least the anticipated height of the peas apart. Do not water the plants unless absolutely necessary before they begin flowering. Then moisture is needed to swell the pods. Too much moisture early on encourages useless growth.

When the seedlings are a few inches high provide support — traditional twiggy pea sticks or netting — or enclose the row with horizontal strings or wires at 15 cm (6 in) intervals. Begin picking the pods when the peas are small, juicy and delicious. Do not wait until they become flat-sided and floury.

Pea varieties grow to different heights and the taller they are, the greater the crop they bear, but the longer they take to mature. For the speediest crop choose a wrinkle-seeded dwarf type, such as 'Little Marvel' or 'Hurst Beagle'. These can be sown in succession throughout the summer if desired. The taller 'Hurst Green Shaft' is an excellent variety to sow at the same time and later. For a late-autumn sowing use a winter-hardy type, such as 'Feltham First'.

Tall peas have gone out of fashion, but in a small area, a 120 cm (48 in) diameter circle of plants of 'Alderman' grown over a wigwam support, can give a very good, prolonged harvest. Although often listed as growing 150 cm (5 ft) high, it usually reaches 180 cm (6 ft) or more.

PEA, SNAP

Sow: spring
Harvest: summer

Unlike garden peas, snap peas have thick fleshy pods, and are eaten pods and all. Picked when young they are completely stringless, and because the pods are removed before the seeds begin to form, the plants keep on flowering and producing more for many weeks. This makes them particularly valuable where space is limited. Their flavour is sweet and similar to garden peas, but not quite the same.

'Sugar Snap' is tall growing and can be grown over a wigwam support. 'Edula' is shorter at about 90 cm (3 ft) high.

POTATO

Plant: early to late spring
Harvest: summer and autumn

A lot of space is needed to become self-sufficient in potatoes, but if you have space it is worth at least growing a row or two of an early variety. Bought ones just do not have the same flavour. The crop is grown from seed tubers planted about 10 cm (4 in) deep in spring. Varieties are divided into earlies, second earlies, and maincrop, according to when they will be ready to harvest. The biggest problem is potato blight, which in a wet season can decimate the later crops if not controlled.

Potatoes grow well in most soils, but best where it has been well manured. The more open and sunny the site the better. Add fertilizer before planting. If the ground was not manured, old manure or compost can be spread along the base of the planting furrows and the tubers spaced out on top before refilling. Normal spacing is 30 cm (12 in) between tubers and 60 cm (24 in) between rows for early potatoes; 38 cm (15 in) between tubers and 75 cm (30 in) between rows for others. Plant earlies in early spring, others before late spring if possible.

Growth of potatoes can be killed by frost, so draw up the soil to cover early shoots if frost is likely. Later, when all growth is about 23 cm (9 in) high, use a draw hoe to pull up soil from between the rows to form a 15 cm (6 in) high ridge along the rows. This is to prevent swelling tubers from breaking through into the light and turning green, also to protect them from blight spores.

Water early varieties whenever the soil begins to dry out. Do not water other potatoes, unless they suffer from drought, until the tubers begin to form or top growth will be excessive. Thereafter water freely.

Begin lifting early varieties as soon as there are sufficient tubers on each plant to warrant it, and follow on with others. Leave maincrop potatoes for storing until the skins of the tubers set (cannot be easily rubbed off with thumb pressure) then lift and store.

Potatoes vary in colour, texture and flavour and some do better on different soils than others. It is a matter of trial and error to find which suits your requirements. Early varieties 'Accent' and red-skinned 'Rubinia' are well worth a trial. 'Desirée', also red-skinned, is a good all-round variety for storing that seems to do well on all soils.

RADISH, SUMMER

Sow: early spring to late summer
Harvest: late spring to autumn

This is the fastest growing salad crop, being ready in three weeks from sowing in summer. Quality is best where the soil is moisture-retentive and the roots develop quickly without a check to growth.

Sow the seeds thinly in close-spaced rows. Weed and water when necessary and control flea beetles by dusting the seedlings with derris in hot, dry weather. First sowings can serve as markers along the same drills as slow-to-germinate seeds. Later they can be fitted in anywhere convenient, such as between rows of newly planted brassicas. Sow at least fortnightly in summer to maintain a succession.

Begin harvesting as soon as the roots are large enough to eat. Many varieties become pithy and hot tasting if left too long.

The normal cropping season can be expanded by sowing under cloches in late winter and early autumn.

'Pontvil' has longish, oval, white-tipped, red roots of very good quality. 'Cherry Belle' and 'Prinz Rotin' have round red roots that hold their quality much longer than old varieties and are still edible when 2.5 cm (1 in) across. Use 'Ribella' for very early sowings, when ordinary summer varieties tend to make too much leaf growth.

RADISH, WINTER

Sow: mid to late summer
Harvest: autumn and winter

These are entirely different to summer radishes, making much larger roots and standing for months without spoiling. Sow thinly in drills spaced 30 cm (12 in) apart and thin the seedlings to 15 cm (6 in) apart. Grow 20 cm (8 in) apart each way in intensive beds.

Lift roots for use as required in autumn and winter. Roots can also be lifted and stored in boxes of sand or peat.

Roots of 'Black Spanish Round' grow 7.2–10 cm (3–4 in) across and are black skinned. Those of 'China Rose' are rosy red and dumpy, some 5 cm (2 in) wide and 12.5 cm (5 in) long. Both these varieties have white flesh and a very pungent flavour. 'Mino Early' is a white radish with cylindrical roots some 5 cm wide and 38 cm long. It is very mild flavoured, crisp and delicious. All are easy to grow.

RHUBARB

Plant: autumn
Harvest: spring

Rhubarb is a large herbaceous perennial grown for its leaf stalks, or sticks — the green leaves are poisonous. It enjoys rich, well-manured soil and a place in full sun for preference. When well fed the plants crop for four to five years, then need to be replaced with fresh ones raised from divisions.

Plant divisions in autumn, setting them 90 cm (3 ft) apart and just deep enough for their large buds to be covered 2.5 cm (1 in) deep. Container-grown plants can be set out in spring.

Mulch the soil around the plants each spring with manure or garden compost if possible, otherwise work in a dressing of fertilizer. Clear away the old growth when it dies down in autumn.

Divide old plants by digging up the crowns, then slicing them into sections with the aid of a sharp spade. Use outer portions, each with at least one or two fat buds, for replanting.

Allow the plants one year's full growth before taking any sticks, so harvesting begins in the second spring after planting. Pull off the largest leaves as required, but always leave four or five on each plant.

Continue gathering the leaves over a period of about six weeks, when the plants should be allowed to grow naturally to build up strength. Remove any flowering stems as soon as you notice them.

An earlier crop can be had by covering a plant or two with upturned boxes, deep buckets or dustbins in winter, and surrounding these with straw or other litter to help keep them warm which will gently force the new growth. The best cover is a purpose-made rhubarb pot with a lid that allows easy inspection and picking.

Forced rhubarb has no green chlorophyll to mask the glorious colour of the stems. Once the uncovered plants begin to crop, remove the covers and allow the forced ones to develop normally and recover.

Specialist firms offer a number of varieties. 'Cawood Delight' has maroon-red leaf stalks and is worth growing for the colour it adds to the plot, but is not suitable for forcing. 'Timperley Early' is very early and of superb colour when forced. 'The Sutton' is a late variety with thick red sticks.

SALSIFY AND SCORZONERA

Sow: spring
Harvest: autumn and winter

To me, at least, both these root crops have the same distinctive, delicious flavour, and are grown the same way, but whereas the roots of salsify are parsnip-like, those of scorzonera are slimmer and black-skinned.

Ideal soil is deep and well manured for a previous crop, but they do well in most gardens given plenty of sun. Sow the seeds thinly along drills spaced 30 cm (12 in) apart and later thin to 15 cm (6 in). Alternatively space sow groups of 3 seeds about 20 cm apart each way in intensive beds.

Lift the roots as required from mid autumn until they begin to grow again in spring.

There does not seem to be much difference between the varieties offered. In any case most seedsmen offer only one of each.

SEAKALE BEET AND RHUBARB CHARD

Sow: spring and mid summer
Harvest: most of year

Seakale beet is a member of the beet family. It produces very large, usually dark green leaves with wide, white, succulent stalks. The green part can be cooked alone or with the chopped stalks like spinach, or the stalks can be braised as a separate dish. Young leaves can be chopped raw for salads.

Seakale beet succeeds in any average garden soil granted a reasonable amount of sun, but does best in well-manured soil. Space sow the seeds 30 cm (12 in) apart or sow thinly and thin to this distance. Allow 45 cm between rows.

Harvest by picking a few leaves from each plant as required. The main picking season is summer from the spring sowing, autumn to spring from the summer sowing. A nitrogen dressing in late winter will improve spring growth.

Rhubarb chard is a closely related plant and most colourful. The leaves are similar, more crinkled and purplish green but its glory is the brilliant red stalks. It can be eaten in the same way, or just admired for its appearance.

The varieties with the largest leaves are dark green 'Fordhook Giant' and pale green 'Lucullus'. Rhubarb chard is usually listed together with seakale beet.

SHALLOT

Plant: winter to early spring
Harvest: mid summer

This is one of the easiest crops to grow. Simply plant single bulbs to half their depth in prepared soil at any time from mid winter to early spring. Then lift the new clusters of bulbs when they ripen in summer.

Shallots do well in most gardens given a sunny site. Space the seed bulbs 15 cm (6 in) apart, leaving 30 cm (12 in) between rows. Make a small planting depression rather than push the bulbs down into the soil surface, which lessens the chance of the developing roots pushing them out again.

Lift the crop when the tops begin to yellow, then dry in the same way as onions before storing them. Provided the plants are healthy, some bulbs can be used for planting the following season, but after saving your own for three seasons, it is then wise to buy new stock.

Yellow shallots keep much longer than the red varieties and are best for general culture. 'Giant Long Keeping Yellow' is reliable and makes a good percentage of large bulbs.

A standard-trained gooseberry makes a novel and productive feature for an ornamental kitchen garden.

SPINACH

Sow: early spring to late spring and early autumn
Harvest: spring and summer

Although in theory it is possible to maintain a succession of summer spinach for months, it tends to run quickly to seed in hot, dry weather, or if its growth is checked in any way, particularly for lack of moisture. Most gardeners therefore restrict sowings to the spring. It is also possible to sow a winter-hardy variety in late summer to overwinter and provide early pickings in spring.

Summer spinach plants are never very heavy cropping but are quick growing and can be used for catch cropping. They do best in rich, moisture-retentive soil in an open site. Sow the seeds along drills spaced 30 cm (12 in) apart. Allow 15 cm (6 in) between the seedlings when thinning, which should be done as soon as possible. Later cut alternate plants to eat when their leaves begin to touch. Keep the crop well watered. Harvest from the remaining plants by regularly gathering a few large leaves from each in turn.

'Norvak' is very reliable and provides pickings over a long season. It is also suitable for an early autumn sowing to overwinter. 'Symphony' and 'Sigmaleaf' are also worthy varieties.

SPINACH, NEW ZEALAND

Sow: late spring
Harvest: summer early autumn

New Zealand spinach is a quick-growing, half-hardy plant with soft, succulent leaves. It is not related to true spinach in any way, nor does it taste like it. However, it does succeed in drier situations where it would be impossible to grow summer spinach.

The ideal spot is a place in full sun. Soak the large seeds overnight before sowing in late spring or early summer. Sow them in twos or threes about 75 cm (2½ ft) apart where each plant is required and later thin to one. Alternatively raise in small pots under glass and plant out when danger of late frost is over.

Pinch out the plants' tips when they have made six leaves; they then spread as a mat to cover the soil.

Harvest by picking the shoot tips, which encourages more shoots to appear, or by plucking individual leaves. No named varieties of this vegetable are offered and it is usually listed as 'New Zealand' under spinach.

SPINACH, PERPETUAL

Sow: spring and mid summer
Harvest: most of year

Perpetual spinach is a form of beet grown for its green leaves. It is easy to grow and a good stand-by when other greens are in short supply. Two sowings — one in spring and another at mid summer — should give a good supply almost the year round. Alternatively, make a single sowing in spring.

Allow 38 cm (15 in) between rows if more than one. Space sow the seeds or thin out the seedlings to 30 cm (1 ft) apart.

Gather the leaves by detaching them from the crown so they come away cleanly. Take a few from each plant at a time.

This usually has no particular variety name and is often found under 'Beet Spinach'.

SWEET CORN

Sow or plant: late spring or early summer
Harvest: late summer, early autumn

This is a form of maize selected for the succulence and flavour of the immature cobs which are picked and eaten. The plants are wind pollinated and need to be grown in blocks instead of rows. Pollen is produced by the 'tassels' at the tops of the stalks, which has to reach the 'silks' at the ends of the cobs.

Under glass, plants are best raised by sowing pairs of seeds in peat pots. Remove one seedling if both germinate. Acclimatize the plants to outdoor conditions before planting them out 45 cm (18 in) apart.

Outdoors, sow two seeds where each plant is to grow and thin out to one where necessary. If covered with cloches, seeds can be sown a week or two earlier.

Harvest the cobs for eating when the sap within the grains is creamy and neither milky nor cheesy. It takes practice to recognize the correct stage from the feel of the cobs, but this can be checked by pulling back the covering sheath and breaking one of the central grains with your thumb nail.

With few exceptions the varieties offered change frequently. 'John Innes Hybrid' is an old and reliable favourite for early cropping. 'Sunrise' is a newer favoured early variety, while 'Sundance' is noted for performing well in poor summers. The 'extra sweet' varieties, such as 'Xtra Sweet Improved' and 'Sweet Nugget' have to be grown in isolation, since if they cross pollinate with another variety their special sweet flavour, for which they are grown, is lost.

TOMATO

Sow: early spring
Plant: late spring or early summer
Harvest: mid summer to early autumn

Tomatoes grown outdoors always have the best flavour. They are also an easy crop to produce, though in cold, wet summers care must be taken to control potato blight. Easiest to grow are bush tomatoes which require no staking or training. The plants need to be raised in warmth and, lacking a heated greenhouse, most gardeners prefer to buy plants rather than try to raise from seed.

Tomatoes do best in rich, well drained soil and must have a sunny, warm site. A place beside a sunny wall or fence is best for those trained up stakes. Space them 38–45 cm (15–18 in) apart in a line. Bush varieties need room to spread and should be set 45–60 cm (18–24 in) apart in a bed. Covering them with cloches at first gives them the best possible start.

Standard (or cordon) varieties must be tied to canes or stakes as their stems lengthen. Also, pinch out all side shoots that appear. Once four trusses (clusters) of flowers have developed, cut off the top of the main stem. Sever it just above the second leaf beyond the fourth truss.

Liquid feed all tomato plants regularly once the first fruits begin to swell, using a high potash fertilizer. Tuck straw or black polythene sheeting under bush tomatoes to keep their fruits off the soil. Gather the fruits as they ripen from mid summer onwards.

It is essential to choose varieties suitable for outdoor culture. 'Outdoor Girl' is one of the earliest to ripen. 'Histon Early' is a little later but of better quality. 'Marmande' is a beefsteak type with very large, fleshy fruits, while 'Gardener's Delight' produces a very large crop of small, very well flavoured tomatoes.

Of the bush varieties 'Red Alert' is very early. Its fruits are small but delicious and peel very easily. 'Sleaford Abundance' is very heavy cropping, but the flavour is not as good as that of some others. 'Red Dawn' is notable as the first bush beefsteak type bred for growing outdoors.

TURNIP, SUMMER

Sow: early spring to mid summer
Harvest: late spring to autumn

Although in theory, quick-growing summer turnips can be grown over a long season, summer sowings will only be successful in humus-rich soil capable of holding plenty of moisture. In most gardens they either bolt or become very coarse. Spring sowings, however, should provide no difficulty granted an open site and fertile soil.

Turnips belong to the brassica family and should not be grown on very acid soil. They are also subject to club root disease and attack by cabbage root fly.

Sow the seeds very thinly along rows spaced 30 cm (12 in) apart. Thin out the seedlings to 23 cm (9 in) apart to allow space for their ample foliage. Under intensive culture allow 23 cm (9 in) each way.

Watch out for flea beetle damage and dust the rows with derris when necessary. Never allow the soil to become more than moderately dry and begin pulling as soon as the roots are large enough to use, when they will be crisp and 'nutty' and can be eaten cooked or raw.

'Snowball Early White Stone' is quick growing and very reliable. 'Purple Top Milan' has purple shoulders and makes a change. You are unlikely to want to grow more than one type.

TURNIPS, WINTER

Sow: mid summer
Harvest: autumn and winter

This crop is sown about mid summer to provide roots to lift and eat as required in autumn and early winter. They can be split by hard frosts so remaining roots are best lifted and stored like carrots before danger of any really hard weather is likely.

Sow in rows spaced 38 cm (15 in) apart and thin the seedlings to 30 cm (12 in) — the plants make a lot of leaf growth and space must be allowed for this. If necessary, dust the rows with derris as soon as the seedlings appear as this will help to control flea beetles. Begin harvesting roots for use as soon as they are large enough to warrant it.

Two of the best winter turnip varieties are 'Golden Ball', with yellow flesh, and 'Manchester Market Green Top Stone' with green shoulders and white flesh.

Herb Guide

Herbs range from shrubs and perennial plants to annuals that are raised afresh each year from seed. Many come from the Mediterranean region and need well-drained soil and plenty of sun, especially those that are shrubs or have silver foliage. This group includes some, like rosemary, that are only partially hardy in temperate zones.

Herbs that are herbaceous — die down in winter and reappear the following spring — generally appreciate much the same conditions as ordinary border plants and are usually handsome enough to warrant a place there.

Those grown from seed each year are normally fitted into the kitchen garden, though parsley can be used to create a neat border edging, and borage can make a pleasant show anywhere with its blue flowers.

BALM, LEMON

(*Melissa officinalis*)

An easy to grow perennial plant reaching to 90 cm (36 in) high. When crushed the leaves emit a powerful lemon scent and can be used for flavouring.

Can be grown in flower border or vegetable plot. Periodically old plants need to be lifted and divided, saving young outer portions for replanting.

Golden balm, M. *o.* 'Aurea' has golden leaves and is shorter. It is much more attractive than the green form, and can be used the same way.

BORAGE

(*Borago officinalis*)

This is an annual that will grow anywhere in sun, its bristly stem rising to 60 cm (24 in) tall and bearing clusters of blue flowers throughout summer. Its stems and leaves can be used in cool drinks or salads, the flowers for decoration.

Sow seeds in spring and thin the seedlings to about 30 cm (12 in) apart.

CHERVIL

(*Anthriscus cerefolium*)

Chervil, which is grown from seed, is a part of the traditional 'fines herbes' and often used in place of parsley. Sow thinly along very short rows several times from spring onwards to provide a succession. Once the foliage is 10–15 cm high begin cutting the plants with scissors about 2.5 cm above soil.

The soil must be well drained, and some shade is often better in summer. A late summer sowing in full sun, thinned to around 23 cm (9 in), gives something to pick in autumn and spring.

CHIVES

(*Allium schoenaprasum*)

An easily grown perennial member of the onion family. Growing some 15 cm (6 in) high it can make a neat edging. If the 'grassy' foliage is not continually cut back — the normal way of harvesting — the plants make a fine show of mauve flowers in summer.

Chives like plenty of humus, a fairly rich soil and moisture. The leaves die down when frosts arrive, but appear again early in spring. Split up the clumps every year or two to prevent overcrowding. They can also be grown from seed sown in spring.

CORIANDER

(*Coriandrum sativum*)

Both the fresh green leaves and the dried seeds of this herb are used. It is unfussy about soil, but for seed production allow it full sun. For green leaves sow thinly in short rows from spring onwards. Cut the seedlings with scissors when growth is 10–15 cm (4–6 in) high. For a harvest of seeds, sown in a patch, thin the seedlings to about 20 cm (8 in) apart and leave to flower.

CURRY PLANT

(*Helichrysum angustifolium*)

This is a shrubby perennial with silvery-white leaves and tiny petal-less yellow flowers in late summer. On hot days it

Canes linked with string or wire can be used to provide temporary support for training trailing cucumbers.

emits a delicious savoury aroma. The mild-flavoured leaves can be included in salads, or a sprig used to flavour a roasting chicken, but it is usually grown for its appearance.

The curry plant needs well-drained soil and plenty of sun. Propagate from cuttings of shoots taken in late summer and rooted in a frame or greenhouse.

DILL
(*Anethum graveolens*)

Dill is an annual easily grown from seed, but its treatment depends on what you want — green leaves or seeds. For a supply of green growth, sow the seeds thinly along short rows every three or four weeks from spring onwards. Begin cutting with scissors once the seedlings are 10–15 cm (4–6 in) high.

For seeds, sow over a patch of ground and thin out to 15 cm (6 in). The plants grow about 90 cm (36 in) high and help support one another. The dull yellow flower heads are quite attractive.

FENNEL
(*Foeniculum vulgare*)

This is a perennial plant with attractive green, ferny foliage and refreshing aniseed aroma. The stems reach upwards of 90 cm (36 in) high and are topped with yellow flowers in late summer. Even more striking is the bronze-leaved form. Both are easily raised from seed sown in spring. Old plants can be divided in spring.

LEAF CELERY
(*Apium graveolens*)

This is much hardier than ordinary celery and makes more leaf than stalk. It can be used from a young age for flavouring.

Choose a well-manured patch of well-drained soil in a sunny site. Sow the seeds outdoors or under glass in spring. Plant or thin out the seedlings 20 cm (8 in) apart and keep them moist. Begin gathering the leaves as required some four weeks later. Height is about 30 cm (12 in).

LOVAGE
(*Levisticum officinalis*)

When grown in deep, fertile soil and given plenty of moisture, lovage grows upwards of 90 cm (6 ft) tall and needs siting with care. It can be disappointing where the soil is poor or excessively dry in summer. The young growth has a delicious smokey-celery flavour.

New plants can be raised from seed sown outdoors, or division of old plants, in spring.

MARJORAM
(*Origanum vulgare*)

Marjoram, or pot marjoram, is a hardy herbaceous plant growing about 60 cm (24 in) high. It prefers light soil and sun and grows happily in the same spot for many years. Use it in any recipe calling for origano, in bouquet garni for soups etc. and in salads.

Plants can be raised from seed, by taking cuttings or, in spring, by taking rooted offsets — small pieces with roots attached — to plant out.

Far more ornamental, and just as effective for flavouring, is its golden-leaved counterpart, golden marjoram (*O. v.* 'Aureum'). This makes a weed-defying dome about 30 cm (12 in) high of bright yellow leaves.

MARJORAM, SWEET
(*Origanum majorana*)

This is grown as a half-hardy annual, by raising the seedlings under glass in spring and either planting them outdoors in late spring or early summer, or growing them on in containers. Height is about 30 cm (12 in). There is also a purple-leaved form which is very attractive. The leaves can be used for flavouring many dishes.

MINT
(*Mentha*)

The mint customarily grown for mint sauce is spearmint, *Mentha viridis*, though some people claim that apple mint, *M. rotundifolia* is superior. There are, however, other mints grown for their appearance.

Most mints reach about 45–60 cm (18–24 in) high at flowering time, apple mint around 90 cm (36 in). All are herbaceous and disappear over winter.

Mints like rich soil, some shade and plenty of moisture. They quickly spread and can become a nuisance unless confined by a barrier in the soil. For a small amount simply sink a bottomless plastic bucket to its rim to prevent the roots wandering. To contain a larger area bury a 30 cm (12 in) wide strip of heavy gauge polythene on edge around the perimeter.

Replant in fresh soil every two or three years. Extract some pieces of healthy young roots about 10 cm (4 in) long to start off again, burying them horizontally 5 cm (2 in) deep in early spring.

NASTURTIUM
(*Tropaeolum majus*)

Nasturtium leaves and buds can be used in salads and the

seeds pickled like capers, but they are one of the longest flowering hardy annuals and make a brave show of their red and yellow blooms.

Sow the large seeds individually 1 cm (½ in) deep in spring. Once up the seedlings are resistant to drought and soon come into flower, continuing until frost arrives.

PARSLEY

(*Petroselinum crispum*)

Parsley is a biennial plant, but it is best to make two sowings each year to maintain a supply. The first sowing, in spring, provides pickings through summer into autumn. A second sowing at mid summer will give plenty of fresh young foliage in autumn and again the following spring.

Growth is killed by hard winter weather, but a cloche placed over a few plants will ensure a winter supply.

POT MARIGOLD

(*Calendula officinalis*)

One of the hardiest of annuals, pot marigolds make a brilliant show of orange flowers and usually self seed. The petals can be used as a food colouring or for decorating salads, and the flowers bring cheerful colour to a kitchen garden.

Sow seeds outdoors in spring where the plants are to grow.

ROSEMARY

(*Rosmarinus officinalis*)

The evergreen, shrubby rosemary needs well-drained soil and, away from mild areas, shelter from cold winds. It makes a fine display of blue or white flowers in late spring.

There are a number of forms varying from upright to spreading and most grow about 60–80 cm (24–32 in) tall. They can be propagated from shoot cuttings taken and rooted under glass or indoors in spring, but the easiest way is to layer a convenient low-placed shoot in the soil beside the bush.

SAGE

(*Salvia officinalis*)

Common sage is a shrubby, evergreen plant. It needs well-drained soil and a warm, sheltered spot. The common kind is easily raised from seed sown under glass in spring. In summer the plants make a bold splash of colour when they flower. More attractive looking in the garden are the purple-leaved sage, *S. o.* 'Purpurascens', and golden-variegated 'Icterina'.

Sages become straggly after a few years and then need to be replaced. Raise new plants by taking cuttings of shoots in mid to late summer.

SAVORY

(*Satureia*)

Summer savory, *Satureia hortensis* is an annual plant easily raised from seed sown outdoors in spring in a sunny spot. It grows 30 cm (12 in) high, has tiny aromatic leaves and is spangled with minute flowers in summer.

Winter savory, *Satureia montana* is an evergreen perennial and available fresh the year round. It reaches the same height and prefers a light, well-drained soil and plenty of sun. When grown as an edging, clip it tidy in spring. Plants can be raised from a spring sowing outdoors.

TARRAGON, FRENCH

(*Artemisia dracunculus*)

French tarragon is the one to grow for cookery and can be obtained from specialist firms. The tarragon seed normally offered is Russian tarragon and is useless for flavouring.

This herb is fussy in its needs for well-drained, light soil, full sun and winter protection. Replant some of the underground runners, which offer a ready means of increase, to a fresh site every third or fourth spring.

French tarragon grows roughly 60 cm (24 in) high. The leaves are pale green and narrow and its flowers are dowdy daisies without petals. It is not a plant for looks, but for anyone who takes cooking seriously it is a must.

THYME

(*Thymus vulgaris*)

Garden thyme forms a low-growing, spreading bush and makes a good display with its mauve flowers in early summer. Good drainage and sun are essential for it to thrive. It can be used as a neat edging, but needs to be replaced after about four years.

New plants can be raised from seed sown outdoors, or by layering shoots in the soil beside the plants. Shoot cuttings can also be taken in summer and rooted under glass.

Lemon thyme, *Thymus citriodorus*, also has culinary uses and can be grown similarly, but it is worth including its golden-leaved form for looks alone. Growing some 15 cm (6 in) high it forms a yellow weed-defying carpet with its aromatic foliage.

Fruit Guide

SOFT FRUITS

Soft fruits should be fed each spring with a dressing of a general balanced fertilizer and/or spreading a thick mulch of well-rotted manure or garden compost over their root areas. Gooseberries and currants often need extra potash, especially on light soils, which can be supplied with a dressing of sulphate of potash. Water the soil in dry periods, especially when the fruits are swelling. Pick the fruit once fully ripe.

BLACKBERRY AND HYBRIDS

This group includes loganberry, tayberry and other hybrids that make long canes every year. They carry fruit on one-year-old canes, thus the shoots that develop one season produce berries in the following season.

Varieties

Planting distance varies according to vigour of variety and few gardeners have room for more than one or two. Of particular interest for small gardens are the blackberry 'Oregon Thornless' and the 'Thornless Loganberry', both of which are easy to handle and do not hook on to clothes. 'Boysenberry' withstands drought better than most and is particularly useful on lighter soils. 'Tayberry' for milder areas, and 'Tummelberry' are also moderate growers. Apart from 'Oregon Thornless' which needs 3 m (10 ft) in which to spread itself, the others mentioned can be planted 2.4 m (8 ft) apart.

RED AND WHITE CURRANTS

Red currants and the white varieties are easily trained as cordons or fans. A cordon can be a single upright stem, or two to four stems springing from low down and trained upright 38 cm (15 in) apart, like a toasting fork.

Varieties

Of the red varieties, 'Johnkheer van Tets' is early to ripen and very heavy cropping. Try this if you have room only for a plant or two. 'Stanza', another heavy cropping variety which ripens a little later, can be added to lengthen the picking season. 'White Versailles' is a widely available and reliable white currant.

GOOSEBERRY

Because their fruits can be picked and cooked when green, gooseberries offer the earliest fruit pickings of the season. Harvesting begins when the berries become large enough to use. If at that stage they are thinned to about 10 cm (4 in) apart, those left will continue to swell and give a second harvest of ripe dessert fruit in summer.

Like red currants, gooseberries can be trained as fans or cordons but are a little more difficult to deal with owing to the fact they are thorny and their shoots are more brittle.

Varieties

If you require gooseberries only for cooking, then 'Invicta' is the best choice. It is very heavy cropping and so far seems to be immune to mildew infection which can be a scourge in some areas. 'Jubilee' is a good dual-purpose variety and one of the heaviest cropping. At maturity the berries are yellow. 'Whinham's Industry' is a red variety, vigorous and does well on most soils. Its flavour is excellent, but it is subject to attacks of mildew.

TREE FRUITS

Feed fruit trees each spring with a general balanced fertilizer. Cooking apples and all plums may need extra nitrogen. Water if necessary during dry spring and summer spells and especially when the fruits are swelling.

APPLES AND PEARS

Trained as cordons, a large number of different apples and pears can be grown in quite a

It is worth experimenting with many oriental vegetables, like chop suey greens, for a wider variety of delicious flavours.

small space. Espalier trees give a much larger crop, but also need more room, depending on the rootstock the trees have (Table 1). Step-over trees are useful as edgings in large kitchen gardens.

Apple Varieties

It is not uncommon for specialist suppliers to offer 50 or more varieties and most gardeners have their favourites. Some of the more reliable dessert ones noted for flavour include 'Epicure' (late summer), 'Fortune' (early autumn), 'Lord Lambourne' (autumn), 'Sunset' (mid autumn/early winter), 'Spartan' (mid autumn/late winter) and 'Sturmer Pippin' (winter/early spring).

Good culinary varieties include: 'Grenadier' (late summer/early autumn), 'Bountiful' (late summer/mid winter) and 'Lane's Prince Albert' (winter/to early spring).

Pear Varieties

Fewer pear varieties are offered than apples, but the following are suitable for a small plot, crop well and have good flavour. 'Beth' (early autumn), 'Onward' (mid/late autumn), 'Conference' (autumn), and 'Glou Morceau' (early/mid winter) which is best against a sunny wall. To these could be added 'William's Bon Chrétien' (early autumn), which has many virtues, but is highly susceptible to scab disease and must be sprayed.

PLUMS

Plums do well in most soils provided they are not badly drained in winter. They tend to make sizeable trees, but can be kept very compact when trained as fan trees.

Varieties

There are a number of self-fertile plums that will crop when grown alone, but the best for a small garden is 'Victoria' (late summer), a good dual-purpose variety that can be cooked or eaten as dessert. If you have space for more than one, 'Opal' (late summer), 'Denniston's Superb' (late summer), that does well in the north of Britain, 'Oulin's Golden Gage' (late summer) and 'Marjorie's Seedling' (dual purpose, early autumn) are worth considering. Should the site be warm and sunny, 'Cambridge Gage' (early autumn) can also be added to the list. 'Pershore Yellow' (late summer), is an excellent and reliable, self-fertile, cooking variety.

SECTION III

APPENDIX I

Season Conversion Table

	NORTHERN HEMISPHERE	SOUTHERN HEMISPHERE
Early winter:	December	June
Mid winter:	January	July
Late winter:	February	August
Early spring:	March	September
Mid spring:	April	October
Late spring:	May	November
Early summer:	June	December
Mid summer:	July	January
Late summer:	August	February
Early autumn:	September	March
Mid autumn:	October	April
Late autumn:	November	May

Where the soil is heavy, raised beds have the advantage of draining more freely; they also save you having to bend down so far.

Herbs like dill and chervil to be used green should be left unthinned and cut with scissors when a few inches high.

Guide to Vegetable Spacings

Vegetable	Between Plants	Between Rows
Artichoke, globe	90–120 cm (36–48 in)	90–120 cm (36–48 in)
Jerusalem	38 cm (15 in)	38 cm (15 in)*
Asparagus pea	45 cm (18 in)	60 cm (24 in)
Bean, broad	20 cm (8 in)	25 cm (10 in)*
French	10 cm (4 in)	45 cm (18 in)
runner	23–30 cm (9–12 in)	30–37 cm (12–15 in)*
Beetroot	10–15 cm (4–6 in)	30 cm (12 in)
Broccoli, sprouting	60–75 cm (24–30 in)	60–75 cm (24–30 in)
Brussels sprouts	75–90 cm (30–36 in)	90 cm (36 in)
Cabbage and Savoy	30–60 cm (12–24 in)	30–60 cm (12–24 in)
Carrot	2.5–5 cm (1–2 in)	30 cm (12 in)
Cauliflower, summer	60 cm (24 in)	60 cm (24 in)
winter	60 cm (24 in)	60 cm (24 in)
Celeriac	30 cm (12 in)	45 cm (18 in)
Celery, maincrop	23 cm (9 in)	25 cm (10 in)*
self-blanching	23 cm (9 in)	23 cm (9 in)
Chicory, forcing	15 cm (6 in)	30 cm (12 in)
heading	30 cm (12 in)	45 cm (18 in)
Chinese Cabbage and Pak choi	30 cm (12 in)	30 cm (12 in)
Corn salad	10 cm (4 in)	10 cm (4 in)
Courgette, Marrow, Squash and Pumpkin — bush varieties	60–75 cm (24–30 in)	60–75 cm (24–30 in)
trailing	60–75 cm (24–30 in)	150+ cm (60+ in)
Cucumber and Gherkin, bush	60–75 cm (24–30 in)	60–75 cm (24–30 in)
trailing varieties	60–75 cm (24–30 in)	120+ cm (48+ in)
Endive	23–30 cm (9–12 in)	30 cm (12 in)
Florence fennel	20 cm (8 in)	30 cm (12 in)
Garlic	15 cm (6 in)	30 cm (12 in)
Kale	60 cm (24 in)	60 cm (24 in)
Kohl rabi	23–30 cm (9–12 in)	30 cm (12 in)
Leek	15–23 cm (6–9 in)	30 cm (12 in)
Lettuce	15–30 cm (6–12 in)	30 cm (12 in)
Onion, maincrop	10–15 cm (4–6 in)	30 cm (12 in)
spring	U	30 cm (12 in)
Parsley, Hamburg	20 cm (8 in)	30 cm (12 in)
Parsnip	15–23 cm (6–9 in)	38 cm (15 in)
Pea, garden	5 cm (2 in)	15 cm (6 in)*
Potato, early	30 cm (12 in)	60 cm (24 in)
maincrop	38 cm (15 in)	75 cm (30 in)
Radish, summer	U	30 cm (12 in)
winter	15 cm (6 in)	30 cm (12 in)
Rhubarb	90–120 cm (36–48 in)	90–120 cm (36–48 in)
Salsify and Scorzonera	15 cm (6 in)	30 cm (12 in)
Seakale beet and Rhubarb chard	30 cm (12 in)	45 cm (18 in)
Shallot	15 cm (6 in)	30 cm (12 in)
Spinach, summer	15–30 cm (6–12 in)	30 cm (12 in)
winter	15 cm (6 in)	30 cm (12 in)
New Zealand	60–90 cm (24–36 in)	60–90 cm (24–36 in)
perpetual	30 cm (12 in)	38 cm (15 in)
Sweet corn	45 cm (18 in)	45 cm (18 in)
Tomato, standard	38–45 cm (15–18 in)	
bush	45–60 cm (18–24 in)	45–60 cm (18–24 in)
Turnip, summer	23 cm (9 in)	30 cm (12 in)
winter	30 cm (12 in)	38 cm (15 in)

Between Double Rows	Intensive Beds: each way between plants
90 cm (36 in)	
60–90 cm (24–36 in)	
	15 cm (6 in)
180 cm (72 in)	
	10 cm (4 in)
	5–8 cm (2–3 in)
	30 cm (12 in)
	18 cm (7 in)
	30 cm (12 in)
	15 cm (6 in)
	20 cm (8 in)
	15–30 cm (6–12 in)
	20 cm (8 in)
	U
	23 cm (9 in)
	23 cm (9 in)
90–120 cm (36–48 in)	
	U
	20 cm (8 in)
	20 cm (8 in)
	18 cm (7 in)
	25 cm (10 in)
	30 cm (12 in)

U *seedlings unthinned;*

* *space between pair of rows forming a double row*

Covering the soil surface with a thick mulch of bark smothers germinating weeds and helps conserve moisture.

Main Vegetable Sowing Times*

Vegetable	Late Winter	Early Spring	Mid Spring	Late Spring	Early Summer
Artichoke, globe				S	
Asparagus Pea				S	
Bean, broad	S	S	S	S	S
French			C	S	S
runner			G	S(C)	S
Beetroot		S(C)	S	S	S
Broccoli, sprouting				S	
Brussels sprouts	C	S	S		
Cabbage and Savoy	C	S	S	S	
Calabrese			S	S	S
Carrot	C	S	S	S	S
Cauliflower, summer	G	S(C)	S		
winter			S	S	
Celery and Celeriac		G			
maincrop		G			
self-blanching		G			
Chicory					S
Chinese cabbage and Pak choi					
Courgette, Marrow, Squash and Pumpkin			G	S(C)	S
Corn Salad					
Cucumber and Gherkin			G	C	S
Endive					S
Florence fennel					S
Kale				S	
Kohl rabi	C	S	S	S	S
Leek		S	S		
Lettuce	C	S	S	S	S
Onion, maincrop	C	S	S		
spring	C	S	S	S	
Parsley, Hamburg			S		
Parsnip		S	S		
Pea, garden	C	S	S	S	S
snap		S	S	S	
Radish, summer	C	S	S	S	S
winter					
Salsify and Scorzonera		S	S		
Seakale beet and Rhubarb chard		S	S		S
Spinach, summer	C	S	S	S	S
winter					
perpetual		S	S		
New Zealand				S(C)	
Sweet corn			G	S(C)	
Tomato	G				
Turnip, summer	C	S	S	S	
winter					

Mid Summer	Late Summer	Early Autumn	Mid Autumn	Early Winter
				S
S				
S				
S				
S				
S				
S				
S	S	S		
S				
S				
S				
S			S	
	S			
	S			
S				
S	S			
S				
S	S			
S				
S				

C under cloches;
(C) cloche cover an advantage;
G in greenhouse or frame;
S sow outdoors
** Do not forget these may vary a little depending on soil, site and where you live*

Main Vegetable Planting Times*

Vegetable	Late Winter	Early Spring	Mid Spring	Late Spring
Artichoke, globe		P	P	
Jerusalem	P	P		
Bean, French				P(C)
runner				P(C)
Broccoli, sprouting				
Brussels sprouts			P	P
Cabbage, autumn and winter				
summer		P	P	P
spring				
Calabrese			P	P
Cauliflower, summer			P(C)	P
winter				
Celeriac				P(C)
Celery				P(C)
Courgette, Marrow, Squash and Pumpkin				P(C)
Cucumber and Gherkin				C
Garlic	P	P		
Kale				
Leek				
Onion, maincrop		P	P	
Potato		P	P	
Rhubarb	P	P		
Shallot	P	P		
Sweet corn				P(C)
Tomato				P(C)

P *plant outdoors;*
C *plant under cloches;*
(C) *cloche cover an advantage*
* *Do not forget that these may vary a little according to soil, site and where you live*

Early Summer	Mid Summer	Early Autumn	Mid Autumn	Late Autumn	Early Winter	Late Winter
						P
P						
P						
P	P					
P	P					
		P	P			
P	P					
P	P					
P						
P						
P						
P(C)						
				P	P	P
P	P					
P	P					
		P	P			
				P	P	P
						P
P						
P						

Sources of Supply

VEGETABLE SEEDS, ONION SETS, ETC.

J. W. *Boyce*, Bush Pasture, Lower Carter Street, Fordham, Ely, Cambs CB7 5JU
D. T. *Brown & Co. Ltd*, Station Road, Poulton-le-Fylde, Blackpool, FY6 7HX
Chiltern Seeds, Bortree Stile, Ulverston, Cumbria LA12 7PB
Samuel Dobie & Son Ltd, Broomhill Way, Torquay, Devon TQ2 7QW
Mr Fothergills Seeds Ltd, Gazeley Road, Kentford, Newmarket, Suffolk CB8 7QB
S. E. *Marshall & Co. Ltd*, Wisbech, Cambs PE13 2RF
Suffolk Herbs (see below)
Suttons Seeds Ltd, Hele Road, Torquay, Devon TQ2 7QJ
Thompson & Morgan, London Road, Ipswich, Suffolk IP2 OBA.
Unwins Seeds Ltd, Histon, Cambridge CB4 4LE

FRUIT TREES AND BUSHES

Chris Bowers & Sons, Whispering Trees Nurseries, Wimbotsham, Norfolk PE34 8QB
Deacons Nursery, Godshill, Isle of Wight PO38 3HW
Highfield Nurseries, Whitminster, Gloucester GL2 7PL
Ken Muir, Honeypot Farm, Rectory Road, Weeley Heath, Clacton-on-Sea, Essex CO16 9BJ

HERB SEEDS

Suffolk Herbs, Sawyers Farm, Little Cornard, Sudbury, Suffolk CO10 0NY
Most vegetable seedsmen also offer a range of herb seeds.

HERB PLANTS

For nearest supplier of herb plants contact:
British Herb Trade Association, Sunnymead, West Pennard, Glastonbury, Somerset BA6 8NN
The Herb Society, 77 Great Peter Street, London SW1P 2EZ

INDEX